# Cloud Time

## The Inception of the Future

# Cloud Time

The Inception of the Future

## Rob Coley & Dean Lockwood

Winchester, UK
Washington, USA

First published by Zero Books, 2012
Zero Books is an imprint of John Hunt Publishing Ltd., Laurel House, Station Approach,
Alresford, Hants, SO24 9JH, UK
office1@o-books.net
www.o-books.com

For distributor details and how to order please visit the 'Ordering' section on our website.

ISBN: 978 1 78099 095 8

A CIP catalogue record for this book is available from the British Library.

Design: Stuart Davies

Printed and bound by CPI Group (UK) Ltd, Croydon, CR0 4YY
Printed in the USA by Edwards Brothers Malloy

We operate a distinctive and ethical publishing philosophy in all
areas of our business, from our global network of authors to
production and worldwide distribution.

# CONTENTS

# Acknowledgements

This book mutated and grew from ideas originally presented at 'The Experimental Society' conference, University of Lancaster, July 2010 and 'Platform Politics', Anglia Ruskin University, May 2011.

# Inception

The focus of our book is on the cultural and political implications of the much vaunted 'cloud computing' phenomenon. Cloud computing, in its most basic terms, is the systematized virtualization of data storage and access, the coalescence of processing power into an instantly available utility, ready for any eventuality. We will, of course, consider certain technical manifestations of the Cloud but, for us, computing is just one component of a cultural, social and political logic. You will be disappointed if you hope for a technical manual. Computational progress, as we understand it, is a kind of alibi for this logic. This discussion, you could say, is conceived as a communiqué from a fictional future in which the world has not been subjected to the straitjacket of capitalist digitality.

So we are much less interested in the technical destiny of the Cloud than in its role in piloting a monstrous new form of power and control. It should be understood as central to the newly *intensive* nature of an already established paradigm of socio-cultural connection and integration, entwined with, but not determined by, emergent technical systems. This culture, defined by the global informatic archive to which we are constantly tethered, fosters a dream-like state in which we can both *possess* and *be* everything we wish *simultaneously*.

All possibilities lay before us. We no longer have to choose. We are encouraged to take on the totality of being. As we contend, this constitutes a collapse of the virtual into the actual – *utopia is actualized* – and reality is defined by a multiplicity of alternatives which forecloses anything beyond or outside itself. 'Cloud culture' promises an explosion of creative potential, yet also ensures that creativity is ceaselessly enclosed in its modulation. Catastrophically, living labor is the engine and the engineer of its enclosure. Moreover, ours is a post-political world, defined by an omnipresent state of 'coalition' and maintenance of 'democratic' consensus that nullifies genuine creativity or transformation, stripping away antagonism. The cooptation of everything into the 'political' results in the disappearance of politics. Politics needs to be dreamed back into existence: we commend a critical immanent delirium of the Cloud, a fabulation spun out from the cramped space into which it installs us.

Those of us whose formative years were, at least partially, wallpapered with Athena posters will remember all too clearly a certain image by M.C. Escher. The image, *Ascending and Descending*, originally a lithograph first printed in 1960, depicts a sect of identical, monkish figures doomed, perhaps coerced, to ceaselessly plod up and down a single, looped set of steps atop an eccentric quasi-gothic building. The image, now of course a cliché, is based upon the conceptual ruse underpinning what are known as 'Penrose stairs'. In the fifties, Lionel and Roger Penrose imagined an impossibility: stairs which, no matter how far or in which direction we proceed, deny us true progress. We turn each corner of the staircase only to find ourselves caught within a closed circuit. Back in the days of Athena, paradox was scarce. That was why the science fiction of a writer such as Philip K. Dick, dealing as it did, in novels such as *Time Out Of Joint* (1959) and *Ubik* (1969), with paranoiac characters prising open fissures unreasonably and sinisterly appearing in consensual reality, still delivered such a powerful impact. However, paradox is now relatively mundane. One of the key themes of our book is the normalization of paradox, the science fictionalization of the world, so to speak, under the aegis of global informational capital. There is a new tendency in mainstream twenty-first century cinema, for example, which has been dubbed 'rubber reality', or, alternatively, 'mind-game film'. Film theorist Thomas Elsaesser suggests that 'rather than "reflecting" reality, or oscillating and alternating between illusionism/realism, these films create their own referentiality, but what they refer to, above all, are "the rules of the game" ... as we learn to live symbiotically with machines and "things", as well as with hybrid forms of intelligence embedded in our many automated systems. In this respect, cinema ... may have become a form of performative agency, as well as a form of thinking'.[1] One such film is Christopher Nolan's near future science fiction film, *Inception* (2010). Criticized for its reduction of dream-states to the dumb exigencies of the action movie or video game, in fact the film is interesting precisely in its insistence on the rationalization of paradox and the logic of dream.

The film concerns the exploits of a team of professional corporate thieves, a finely tailored transnational crew who specialize in extracting lucrative industrial information from their targets' subconscious minds as they sleep. Recruiting bushy-tailed academic, Ariadne (Ellen Page), the team, headed by Dom Cobb (Leonardo DiCaprio), aim on this occasion not to thieve but to plant an idea, in effect a virus, that will infect and inflect the future business decisions of the 'mark', Robert Fischer (Cillan Murphy). The aim of this 'inception' (for it is from this seeding that the film takes its name) is, as Cobb explains, 'to translate a business proposition into an emotional reaction'. Ariadne's task is to construct a 'dream architecture' of affective capture, an oneiric space in which this proposition can be worked in and thereafter manipulated. As such, the team's mission is to lock down and harness the virtuality of the imagination in order to define a moveable, manipulable truth. In this respect, the mental architecture Ariadne must build will be definitively Cartesian (that is, rational and scientistic), and it is surely no coincidence that her tutorial takes place in the avenues and boulevards of Paris, themselves of course the result of the urban rationalization process of mid-nineteenth century Haussmannization (dedicated in part to the closing down of an insurrectionary dream). And yet, the dream architects will retain the power to fold this space in the most Baroque manner, demonstrated as a whole section of the city is rolled back over onto itself to form a loop. What is crucial is that inception is a control strategy that requires the mark to maintain a state of relative autonomy and self-invention. It is a form of control that foregoes the hegemonic mode of 'power over' and shifts into a mode in which power is exerted from 'within', in fact 'owned' by the mark as his very capacity to act in the world and discover his own truth. The mark is enlisted in the process of his own control, his actions are wholly *re*active. In the language of the corporate world from which *Inception* never strays, we can say that he's been *incentivized*. The film's interest, for us, rests in this migration of power into life's interior, the becoming ontological of power.[2]

This rationalization of existence is part of a greater move towards science-as-knowledge, in the form of calculation, process, extrapolation; the management of data to define truth. It engenders a nihilistic oscillation of the will, a 'disjunctive synthesis' of passivity and radicalism.[3] When Cobb and his wife, Mal, become trapped in a dream limbo, possessing absolute creative freedom over this world of the imagination, they merely render a city of dull banality, block after block of vague, generic structures, an existence with minimal detail and texture. The dream is lucid and, as such, ordered, efficient even. Experience, for them, becomes pseudo-experience, no matter how hedonistic and narcissistic. Affect is muted, modulated and narcotized. Our present cultural milieu constitutes a similar state of passive boredom. It seems to lack the *value* by which all things are judged. The ability to have, to be, anything and everything, remains limited by a project of moderation in line with our passive nihilist, decaffeinated culture.[4] We crave extremity but will not countenance pain. Anyone who has ever played a video game in the 'cheat' or 'god' mode knows how quickly initial interest is replaced by ennui, but this is perhaps less a result of the ability to do *anything* within the game-space without being 'killed' and more about the totalizing nature of the space itself, the reduction of the virtual into the actual. Even cheating, it seems, has rules to which we must abide. The crisis brought about in cloud culture is the impossibility of the creative act in this world where everything that has been done is instantly available, everything that is in process is connected, and even that which has yet to occur is part of an endless archive. Of course, for Cobb and Mal, who lay in front of an oncoming train in order to return to 'reality', suicide offers a way out. This hints at the radical twin to what J. G. Ballard has called the 'collaborative soft tyranny' of contemporary nihilism. The other half of our disjunctive synthesis is an 'elective psychopathology,'[5] an immanent antagonism that remains contained while threatening to spill over into fundamentalism. The argument put forth here is that cloud culture constitutes a determined attempt to harness the affective power of this nihilism. The process of rationalization involved in the collapse of the virtual into the actual produces a state of passive disorientation constantly approaching self-destructive despair which lends itself to manipulation and modulation. The fine-tuning of this deadlock results in the continuity and productive stability of contemporary informational capitalism. Correspondingly, Cobb's inception team constantly strives to stay on the right side of precarity, to prevent the complete 'collapse' of the dream-state.

The need to maintain stability can be understood in terms of the politics of *security*, and contemporary capital secures stability precisely through the use of paradox.[6] The space of control is a space of impossible structures. *Inception* contains a set of Penrose stairs which handily illustrate the disjunctive Baroque-Cartesian synthesis described here. Lionel and Roger Penrose actually photographed a model of their stairs. Clearly, the photograph documents a ruse, a piece of theatre. In reality, the four angles of steps never joined up and the success of the photograph hinges upon the precise angle from which it was taken (seemingly influencing the point of view Escher would later adopt in his lithograph). So it is in *Inception*. When one of Cobb's inceptors is chased down stairs designed as security protocol, he impossibly manoeuvres around and behind his pursuer. The power he exerts in this sequence is executed precisely by demonstrating the trick of the structure to his assailant and revealing the deadly drop concealed by 'natural' perspective. 'Paradox', he says, as the assailant plummets into the rift. Fundamentally, this form of security works on the *revision and modulation of truth*; the power to conduct such modulation is the advantage of a wholly integrated cloud culture to advanced informational capitalism. Indeed, the manifesto of a culture predicated on total and permanent connection is one of absolute transparency in which information freely flows. Control over (false) totality, the apparent enclosure of all virtuals, enables that which is defined as truth to be modified and adjusted as necessary in order to maintain or stimulate production. Consequently, this is not just perceived truth but actual truth, to which *there is no alternative*. This occurs not as hierarchical dictat, but as subtle and supple method of control exercised through ontology itself. Cheating still takes place within rule-bound structures, but in this case it is the rules of the game themselves that are subject to change. Importantly, these rules are not amended in ways that deterministically affect us. Instead, we are implicated in the discovery of their transition, the emphasis of our creative efforts shifts, and we *create* the truth through our very *reactions*. Truth, as such, becomes a flexible control method that no longer makes its plea to the transcendental but is collapsed instead into immanence. Just as the nihilistic synthesis of affect is autopoietic, paradoxical security enables the maintenance of a homeostatic equilibrium that is simultaneously productive.

Thematically, *Inception* is aligned to what we will argue is the operating mode of contemporary capitalism, a capitalism-in-mutation which is driven by a will to truth and a desire to enclose and appropriate the virtual, translating the powers of life into business.[7] The mark lives the inception as his inmost truth and compass. Inception accesses and modulates the affective life of our convictions, our giving of form to the world through our personal beliefs and values. As the mark invents his illusion, he enfleshes the truth of a corporate trigger. Inception is the corporate capture and *détournement* of living labor, life's power to differ, its self-overcoming. Any attempt to resist capitalism must take this into account.

# Chapter 1

# The World Rights Itself

*[W]e need to think upside down once again.*
Charles Leadbeater

*How is it that "the world turned upside-down" always manages to*
Right *itself?*
Hakim Bey

## Coding the World

The take-up of digital technologies is conditioned by existing rhetorics and practices. In particular, computing emerged out of the contexts and concerns of war and capitalism, the economic and military imperatives of the twentieth century. In the cybernetic cultural imaginary the rhetorics of technical rationality and order congeal and gather momentum even further. Cybernetics, as initially conceived, is a prophylactic dream of control, of the regulation of flows, a systems theory which is also a fiction predicated upon the evacuation of the evils of chaos, noise, dirt, viral poison.

Technology has been extremely effective at systematically ordering and opening up the world as resource. This is also a rendering of the world as calculable. The power of digitality in particular lies in its giving over of phenomena to numerical, statistical value, permitting the measure and modulation of any variation in their properties. The mediation of all things through binary code evacuates the content the world, translating everything into homogeneous, replicable form, into information. In the Wordsworthian cliché, the digital 'murders to dissect'. It cuts into phenomena as it orders, disambiguating and freezing up dead moments in linearized fashion. Anything that can be formally represented is so ensnared. Anything that refuses to surrender its singularity, its complexity and power of difference needs must be discarded. Digitality constitutes a capture, an articulation of the world in terms of increasing resolution, ever tightened thresholds, but no matter the degree of resolution or the grip of thresholds, something about the world is lost, something that escapes. That is, the creative, unrepresentable power of virtuality, the singular not-yet that moves the actual and forces it to differ.[8]

If first order cybernetics was dominated by an apotropaic mission, second order cybernetics embraced the productive potential of viral pathology, shifting its verdict on noise from unwanted anomaly to facilitator of flexibility and autopoiesis. Viral noise is 'folded in', transformed into 'constructive instability', excluded precisely via its inclusion and mobilisation.[9]

Capitalism, like first order cybernetics, can be conceived as preoccupied with hygiene in that it wages war against the noisy, viral evil of singularity. It abstracts all phenomena, rendering in terms of exchange value. All things are equalized, prepared for commodity exchange. Of course, from Marx's perspective, it is a revolutionary and brutal stripping away of veils, knocking off of halos, a fundamental compulsive dislodging of things and agitation of the world. And, so, capital embraces 'revolution'. How hygienic can it ever really be? In fact, its hands are always dirty. Chaos and contagion is fundamental to capital. *The Communist Manifesto* treats the bourgeoisie as a contagion capable of passing through any imaginable prophylactic boundary: 'In one word, it creates a world after its own image'.[10] Capitalism is itself viral. It is metamorphic, evolving, mutating through contagion. It 'codes the world according to its own image'.[11] Digitally reconfiguring the world by means of networked power, it conquers through viral ontology.

Capital is complicit with second order cybernetic systems.

What this book is about, at core, is capital's radical autopoietic strategy for harnessing digitality in order to breach the not-yet, capital's predaceous inclinations towards time-out-of-joint, to insert itself into the virtual and take the future in hand. We argue that the Cloud constitutes digital capital's best effort at the in(ter)ception of the future.

## Cloud Enclosure

What would the CEOs of the IT industry, digitally turned-on politicians, media pundits and technology journalists, have us believe the Cloud is? The Cloud basically refers to the abstraction and 'virtualization' of computing. It is based upon an 'as-a-service' model, much like a utility on demand. The end user draws on whatever is needed (infrastructure, platform or software) precisely as it is needed, from whichever device they have in hand, rather than owning hardware or installing software in their machine. Cloud computing constitutes a shift from desktop computing on PCs to computing online via a multiplicity of hosts and platforms. The 'computer', increasingly likely to be a smartphone, tablet or similar device, will continue to run various apps or a web browser, but all computing processes and data storage will occur at remote, virtual servers. Minimal local storage, minimal local processing power. In the Cloud model, all the drudge and unpleasantness of dealing with computers – from the point of view of end users – will be outsourced.

Consumers already use the incipient Cloud, responding to the sheer proliferation of data by storing more and more online. Its primitive form has been familiar to us for some time: user-generated multimedia content and archives, communal 'knowledge', the exchanges of web-based email and blogs, social and communicational networks. But, to take us forward, to bring us the Good News, the technology giants have rolled out their big hitters. Steve Ballmer of Microsoft tells us it's all or nothing –

he's 'bet the company' on the Cloud, while Steve Jobs of Apple promises new kinds of freedom, an 'automatic' and 'effortless' world. Of course, not all of the content in the Cloud is generated by users but it remains open to all, with clear encouragement towards 'creative' engagement. The power of these virtual software solutions – the 'Cloud Power' – is non-linear mass collaborative working, multiplicities of remote users working on the files simultaneously, sharing and developing the ideas together. No messy synchronization or management is required from the user, the Cloud seamlessly – naturally even – integrates disparate devices, users and systems. And the power here is unlimited: in the Cloud, things are only ever more 'flexible', 'scalable'.

So the Cloud responds to the call for collaborative culture already inspired by Web 2.0. It promises enormous potential for project collaboration in both business management and science. Companies are beginning to recognize its value in the context of the global economic recession. It will enable them to focus on their 'core mission', shed staff (namely those who serviced in-house computing), outsource most peripheral concerns and cut costs all round. The total connection of cloud computing, we are told, the state of being 'always on', will push far beyond what we currently understand as interaction. The Cloud, then, is *potential*.

The Cloud has also been understood in terms of the 'digital commons'. In facilitating the storage of our cultural heritage, rendering it increasingly accessible and interactive, it adds up to an 'exponential growth in mass cultural expression' which Charles Leadbeater calls 'Cloud Culture'. In the new decade, he trumpets, 'will come a vast cultural eruption – a mushroom cloud of culture' disrupting 'how culture is expressed and organised'.[12] There's a lot of talk about the 'commons' these days. Not just the commons, in fact: commonism, communalism, new coopera-tivism, indeed, even *communism* is on the agenda. Some of this talk has, understandably, been from those eager (as it transpires, rather too eager) to write the obituary for neoliberalism in the wake of 2008's global financial collapse. But from wherever it manifests, it highlights the growing urgency for new ways of living on an ever more interconnected planet, where the 'crisis' of one country is increasingly the crisis of the world, where individual actions result in a multiplicity of reactions. Discussions around the *digital* commons have, perhaps inevitably, been seen in less significant terms, driven instead by debates over copyright, legality and access. However, the appearance of the Cloud, in socio-political terms, reveals a radical shift already underway in the way we live, a shift that has consequences beyond merely technological concerns.

In early 2010, Leadbeater produced two reports for British think-tanks. In the first of these, 'Cloud Culture: The Future of Global Cultural Relations', we are promised a future of 'mass self expression, ubiquitous participation and constant connection,' a world where our interaction will be driven by 'collaborative learning and improvement'.[13] Leadbeater announces the birth of an exciting new world of invention, creation, innovation and experimentation. Cloud *culture* is defined by its heterogeneity and horizontal connectivity – our interaction with various technologies is presaged as accessible, *open*. Indeed, this is culture as network-of-networks, culture as 'commons'. Here lies the truly utopian essence of the Cloud – indeed, it's a utopia with echoes of Thomas More's original use of the term – no private ownership, no locks on doors (no passwords), an open and collaborative structure. With the common language of information, our communicative and social networks can bring about creativity through commonality. Crucially, then, cloud computing enables – *requires* – our contribution to a global archival system, to which we are correspondingly granted access. But we shouldn't get distracted by the specific technology involved in cloud computing - this can and will change rapidly. The key to cloud *culture* is fundamentally its *integration* and its state of 'always-on'. This integrated-commons forces together existing socio-political, cultural and aesthetic structures, and so has wide-reaching implications.

The nascent utopia Leadbeater presents is, unintentionally, as bizarre a satire as More's island state. And the reason for this must be put down to a central naivety. The only threat to the pending realization of this new creative order, Leadbeater suggests, is a 'cloud capitalism' that may seek to manage, manipulate and dominate our creativity; here he expresses concern over existing web-mammoths such as Facebook and Google, the very definition of informational capitalists in their monetization of interactivity, social networking and search, especially through highly targeted advertising. Yet, in reality, the dangerous possible future of a cloud-based capitalism has not only *already* become fact, but in this contemporary scenario where capital must be recognized as a force of rationalization and control, the Cloud should be understood precisely as both the force behind this new paradigm and its new *configuration*.

What Leadbeater refers to as the 'cloud culture equation' is actually a statement and plan of execution. Like capital itself, the Cloud is processual – in this case a process of integration and archivization. Cloud computing is undoubtedly a central factor, if not apotheosis, of the continuing acceleration of globalization, itself concerned with a 'totalizing' integration of cultural difference within an overall system of control. Yet we're not referring here to the 'single world' of globalization that renders the majority of people locked out from world markets and commodities. The Cloud seeks to align together a complex of worlds in which everything is seemingly open to everyone. This is globalization as cultural assemblage: heterogeneous, 'radically' democratic, yet disembedded, codified and archived in an ultimately homogenous fashion. Data begets data in a newly intensified state of interconnection. The creative explosion Leadbeater promises is beyond even Bill Gates's dreams of a 'friction free' capitalism; here individual meaning and truth are irrelevant outside of the overall assemblage, we become nodal connections, linked to endless alterities. It's for this reason that Leadbeater's insistence that we should 'seek the maximum possible diversity of clouds rather than thinking simply of *the* cloud' utterly overlooks the true extent of this new regime of power.[14] Commercial clouds and social clouds necessarily operate as concrete assemblages piloted by a single 'diagram' or 'abstract machine', to borrow Deleuzian terminology.

We exist, then, in a permanent state of connection, an ontological integration with and through the cloud, brought about via a knowing or unknowing interaction with a multiplicity of devices, augmenting and drawing on the commons. More than this, we simultaneously become embedded within and *a constituent part of* the commons. This commons is an inconceivably vast and ever-expanding data archive but it's also the assemblage of those linked together and mediated by the Cloud. We should thus think of the commons as *virtual*, defined less by existing data and more by its *potential* to produce data through network communication. Consequently, cloud culture harnesses network labor-power,[15] and in so doing dynamically mobilizes what Marx referred to as the 'general intellect': cognitive and social power is transformed into the principle productive force. The commons is certainly comprised of data, codes and information but it's also made up of ideas, notions and concepts, and further, of relationships, connections and affects, all of which exist in both actual and virtual states. Labor in this context is both dialogic and performative; sharing an idea doesn't delimit its value, in the process of its dissemination it is cultivated and enhanced.[16] It goes without saying that the immaterial labor involved in social networking is driven by a chronic requirement for the new and the ceaseless bureaucracy of tagging, (re)categorizing and (re)sorting. A state of constant flux then, where all processes, all actions, are effectively beta-testing – in accessing data, we feed information back to its source where modifications and adjustments take place ahead of our next engagement.

The Patron Saint of cloud culture is Gerrard Winstanley, seventeenth-century founder of the Diggers, an English proto-communist revolutionary group. A resurgence of interest in Winstanley has been evident of late, suggested by a small flurry of reissued writings and several re-examinations by Tony Benn and others. Leadbeater's own assessment appeared little over a month after the publication of 'Cloud Culture', in the form of 'Digging for the Future', a second think-tank report (which he somewhat ambitiously describes as 'an English radical manifesto'). His report hinges upon an anamnesic strategy – we must 'look back to move forward'.[17] The retrospective gaze singles out Winstanley's social radicals as the crucial lesson of the past. Winstanley demanded land be communally owned to foster greater local power. This decentralization and common ownership, he argued, would allow greater efficiency in the culti-vation of the land in order to feed England's growing population, and, further, that in a national process of becoming 'commoners', the people would be levelled, bringing an end to the hegemonic power of priests and landowners.[18] Crucially, common ownership would free up the power of *invention* as driving force for change: 'fear of want and care to pay rent to taskmasters hath hindered many rare inventions'.[19] For Leadbeater, then, the power of Winstanley's ideal of a common land is translatable into a contemporary digital commons, an open network of communal power, a space where knowledge is freely shared for social good, beyond the concerns of capital.

Leadbeater's response to the end-time of the neoliberal project, juxtaposing the cloud commons with this eulogy to Winstanley, overlooks the fact that the digital commons is the new hunting ground for contemporary capital. Cloud culture is a product of post-9/11 'disaster capitalism'. Technological systems and ideas that were in their infancy prior to 9/11, merely 'lying

around' without coherence, were swiftly joined up and rationalized in a way that previously had been politically untenable.
'Suddenly,' Naomi Klein comments, 'the fear of terror was
greater than the fear of living in a surveillance society'.[20] Global
financial meltdown has only served to increase moves toward
greater control through integration. The continuing propagation
of the Cloud occurs in a state of permanent crisis and shock, of
which a deepening sense of nihilism is symptomatic.
Consequently, the state of the digital commons should be further
considered in terms of Klein's reference to the ancient quasi-legal
status of *terra nullius*: the declaration of land as empty or
'wasted' leading to its seizure. As a strategy of land-grabbing
colonial powers, this seizure would often lead to the elimination
of indigenous people 'without remorse', but in the contemporary
case, elimination of invention-power would be counterpro-
ductive. The power of cloud capitalism seeks instead to put us to
work – in this respect, the commons have become subject to
*enclosure*.

## Soft Tyranny

Network structures perpetuate a new, immanent control,
through sets of rules and formulae, codes which pre-format our
actions and behaviors. We will characterize this, as some others
have done, in terms of the logic of video games – 'play' proceeds
in terms of internalizing the code, the protocological and
algorithmic architecture of the game. Thus, for Brian Massumi,
interaction is most commonly found in the context of what he
calls the 'gaming paradigm'. The paradigmatic object of the
video game has been seized upon by informational capitalism as
thoroughly good for business, and is now seen 'massively in
communications, but also in marketing, design, training,
education'.[21] In the interactive gaming paradigm, action is
foregrounded, and, in the two-way traffic between gamer and
algorithmic architecture, *re*action. It is instrumental in its

emphasis, 'backgrounding its own artistic dimension'.[22] For Massumi, interaction is here typically (although not necessarily) associated with a certain 'soft tyranny'. The imperative to participate, to expressively engage with the world as gamespace is very strong, comprising a compulsion to 'become who you are'. Interaction elicits our visceral action. The interactive game encourages us to expose ourselves: 'You are viscerally exposed, like a prodded sea cucumber that spits its guts. You are exposed down to your inmost sensitive folds, down to the very peristaltic rhythms that make you what you are'.[23] This is, of course, productive, generative biopower, power that probes the body's soft innards. In interaction, we are compelled to unfold according to systemic imperatives. In the context of consumption as interactive game, the system responds to our desirous action by modulating and creating anew that desire: 'New needs and desires are created, even whole new modes of experience, which your life begins to revolve around. You have become, you have changed, in interaction with the system. You have literally shopped yourself into being. At the same time, the system has adapted *itself*. It's a kind of double capture of mutual responsiveness, in a reciprocal becoming'.[24] Power exposes our vulnerable soft tissue. It prises out the soft body, including it, holding it within the space of power. Power compels us to reveal our generative tissue, our power of life for its own self-mutating ends. Yet, paradoxically, power draws out the soft tissue only by probing us through the medium of our databased selves.

We need to take a slightly closer look at the character of power as configured in the Cloud to pursue this thought. For Michel Foucault, capitalist accumulation is piloted by a 'disciplinary' diagram of power which emerged, among other ways, in the measures taken to protect towns against the horror of plague. Plague necessitated the freezing of space and the immobilization of populations. Plague was conceived as harboured by the teeming crowd in which bodies indiscriminately mingle. The solution was the abolition of the crowd and the production of the surveilled modern subject. Everything here depended upon a strategy of enclosure, confining wandering bodies in order to render them productive, to register and shape behavior and make them work. In the disciplinary mode, subjects move, observed from one space (or 'mould') to the next. In its various moulds (factories; asylums; schools; prisons; the home, etc.) discipline mass-produces bodies as standardised individuals. It 'cares' for its docile subjects, lending them enduring substance and structure that can be shaped and moved as necessary.[25]

Foucault emphasizes the serial and optical aspects of discipline. Discipline is a vision machine – a panopticon – in which the inspecting gaze never rests, never fails to sweep every inch. However, it is not just a vision machine, it is also a sorting machine. It is about the accumulation of knowledge and the sorting and ordering of this knowledge. In the digital context, this is crucial. With digital archives, databases and networks, observation and administration is greatly facilitated. Increasingly, the emphasis shifts from serial and optical control to modulatory control of data. In this sense, control deals less directly with bodies than with the data patterns that result from such sorting procedures. I am ghosted by my data double – it's not *me*, the individual, that is at issue, it is the non-conscious agency of my data ghost, the 'dividual', as Deleuze puts it. Control modulates bodies; it does not confine and render them static. It is a form of power which works through the manipulation of the flows which move bodies, and the thresholds across which they must cross. As Deleuze puts it, 'in control societies ... the key thing is no longer a signature or number, but a code: codes are *passwords*, whereas disciplinary societies are ruled (when it comes to integration or resistance) by *precepts*'.[26] Easily predicted and manipulated, the data double is more convenient, more efficient all round. It offers the informationalized self, the self stripped of troublesome peculiarities and quirks. The data double, in a sense, ghostwrites us.

Self-consciousness is organisable in a multiplicity of possible ways. For Foucault, the process of subjectivization is the winnowing down to only one. Disciplinary power actualizes one possibility – the individual – and closes down all others. However, as Franco Berardi comments, post-disciplinary subjectivization is less concerned with the 'solidity' of identity than with an environment that is essentially a provisional, ceaselessly transformed chemical composition.[27] The modulatory corporate power we are getting at is a much more fluid organisational form than disciplinary moulding. We have a process of constant modulation, ongoing automatic and networked adjustment according to the patterns of behavior detected. We are predicted, projected and programmed in short order. It is chemistry and the commotion of flow, turbulent fluid, that is subject to management and determines the character of political action.

Foucault has set out the form enclosure took as piloted by what he calls the disciplinary diagram. But, driven by a mutation of capitalism, which in turn is facilitated by and drives digitality, a new diagram of power has been in the ascendant for some time – this is Deleuze's 'monster' of control. Where discipline tries to limit and hedge in the plague of mobility and mutability, to immobilize wandering bodies, control thrives on it and puts it to work. As Deleuze has it in his fragmentary reflections on control society, incarceration is replaced by remote regulation and adjustment, 'ceaseless control in open sites'.[28] Control is 'free-floating' and continuous; Kafkaesque in its 'endless postponement', it never lets us be done with anything. In control society, 'nothing's left alone for long', education and work blur together, 'giving way to frightful continual training', to which we joyfully submit. We can see how control places an enormous premium on securing endless flexibility and malleability of subjects. It never lets up testing our tolerances. Our 'success', as in any video game, hinges upon our ability to divine the underlying algorithmic logic at work and embrace our transformation and flexibilization.

The danger the Diggers posed to established wealth was the active self-organization and surge in militancy of the poor. The enclosure of common land ensued. Rather than controlling the population through spatial enclosure and consequent enforced sedentarism, though, the romanticized, pseudo-hippy mantra of cloud culture (so evident in a spate of recent mobile phone commercials which deliver this rhetoric accompanied by a folk soundtrack and in an 'earthy' colour palette) is keen to paint us as freely-wandering 'nomads'. However, we remain digitally sedentary; evident in GPS tracking – increasingly a standard feature of mobile media – and via the near-invisible RFID chip (Radio-Frequency Identification), present in everything from clothes to food. More significantly, we become subject to the immanent control of *protocol* and *algorithm*, crucial for the organization of network structures.

Protocol is an immanent form of parametric control designed to regulate, flow and direct via underlying structures such as code and passwords. Even a supposedly 'open' commons is replete with such internal structures. Protocol acts *through* information. In this respect, cloud culture brings about the 'informationalization' of life itself: the breakdown of 'life' into constituent binary form, and its permanent storage within databases, consumer profiles and official records, all of which results in an informational indexing of life, distributed throughout the cloud network. '[O]nce life is information', Alexander Galloway and Eugene Thacker suggest, 'and once information is a network, then the network is made amenable to protocols – but with the important addition that this real-time, dynamic management of the network is also a real-time, dynamic management of "life itself" or living networks.'[29]

As intimated before, the algorithmic underpinning of cloud culture can be understood in terms of the operation of video

games. Galloway again: 'Video games don't attempt to hide infor-
matics control; they flaunt it ... The gamer is ... learning, internalizing, and becoming intimate with a massive, multipart, global
algorithm. To play the game means to play the code of the game.
To win means to know the system ... I suggest that video games
are, at their structural core, in direct synchronization with the
political realities of the informatic age.'[30]

Google have been somewhat coy about the intentions of their
search algorithm – 'the holy grail of search is to understand what
the user wants'[31] – but around the time the company launched its
'Google Instant' upgrade, which aimed to generate real-time
'results' to queries that have yet to be completed, Executive
Chairman Eric Schmidt was happy to spell out the intentions of
this algorithm more explicitly: 'I actually think most people don't
want Google to answer their questions ... They want Google to
tell them what they should be doing next'.[32] This is the
motivating force of all algorithmic control. Again, then: video-
game logic, permitting only certain moves to be made, refusing
others. Accordingly, the biopolitics of code is inherent in its
mediating role – something that reduces 'interaction' to *reaction*,
a modulation of our *self-generating* reality. This is what N.
Katherine Hayles calls the *technological nonconscious*: the system
of everyday habits generated and regulated by interactions with
technological devices, a state that, within the network-of-
networks that is cloud culture, is equally apparent in the milieu
of the everyday itself, regardless of direct interaction with a
device.[33] In the film, *Inception*, Cobb and his team effectively
plant an algorithmic control within Fischer's subconscious – a
virtual that will generate an actual.[34] In the context of the Cloud,
the absence of any such masterminding of events from behind a
curtain is only another layer to the paradox. Even the example of
cloud-capitalists such as Google is misleading in this sense – the
complexities of the pervasive codification implanted within the
everyday are so great that no individual, no corporation is

wholly in command. Information capital is a process that has become indistinguishable from the process of life itself. Consequently, invention-power is subject to this coded mediation – the much hyped creative freedom of the commons becomes enclosed, and while communal and communicative production is encouraged, it necessarily occurs within coded boundaries of control. Invention-power itself is enclosed, reduced to a level of reactive creation designed merely to stave off systemic obsolescence and ensure the continual flow of capital.

Leadbeater goes so far as to comment, in an article for *The Observer* which glosses his views on the Cloud, that 'cloud capitalists will want to harvest all they can from their clouds, which means turning you and me, our preferences and interactions into pieces of information to be analysed by algorithms. They will not see us as readers, customers or members, but as bits of linked information'.[35] Business takes its new fluidity or gaseousness for the possession of a soul, but here we face the prospect of reduction to data to be sieved in the sorting machine of post-panoptical pattern recognition and modulation. But what comes first, escape or capture? Can we, in fact, distinguish? Escape or capture: the manuals are available to both friends and foes. Capitalism seizes and mimics escape in order to mutate, it needs its wandering bodies. Capitalism has always had its head in the clouds. Capitalism decodes desire, or rather it engenders proliferation of fluidly coded desire. It is thixotropic, placing its own institutions under stress, stirring up what congeals to set it moving again. It deterritorializes, renders fluid, unleashes desire, but only to recode, to regulate, to sort, sieve, anticipate and modulate by virtue of the technology of control.

## SF Capital

In his postscript on control societies, Deleuze says 'we don't have to stray into science fiction' to find the kind of control mechanisms he outlines.[36] However, isn't it more the case that control emerges precisely as a result of power straying into science fiction? Science fiction deals in virtuals. The radicality of (capitalist) reality is precisely that *capital* has embraced science fiction. It is capital that locks on to the potentiality of events, locks on to the virtual. Capital has become experimental. Thus, 'SF capital', for Mark Fisher, identifies with John Carpenter's *The Thing*, seizing the power and vitality of becoming.[37] This vitality of power should be understood in terms of a new post-hegemonic order. The Thing doesn't supervise, doesn't so much exert power *over*, in the sense of domination or instrumental *potestas*. It has migrated inside invention and self-creation. Again, we are increasingly 'constituted from the inside' by the order of power.[38]

'There is no longer a ruling class', Fisher comments, 'but a Control or Management class which is itself first of all Controlled and Managed, not by transcendent laws, but by immanent circuits, in which "everyone" "participates", but for whom "no-one" is responsible, and whose products "no-one" wants'. There is no distinguishable centre of control, just as there is no distinguishable moment of consumption in a context in which capitalism has sunk so deeply into life: 'The hyper-commodity is not an object, but an intricate, microsensitive, semiotic web, inducing participation and "involvement"'. We are now past the moment when promotion and advertising can be separated from the product, the commodity. We play the hyper-commodity and as we play it we both buy and sell hype. Consider the case of Nine Inch Nails' supremo Trent Reznor's 2007 *Year Zero* project – yes, an album was released, but only as one strand in a web which involves the consumer in a full-blown alternate reality game (ARG, a game which involves gathering information both online and offline and which obscures the difference). Based on the concept of a near-future dystopian America in which Christian Fundamentalism reigns victorious, cracking down on terrorism through brutal erosion of freedoms and declaring the nation reborn, the ARG began with messages embedded in the design of tour t-shirts and then a wave of 'subversive' websites, ostensibly as warnings transmitted to 2007 from the future chaos of Year Zero. USB drives holding further clues were also left in the toilet stalls at concert venues for fans to discover. Videos appeared on YouTube. Reznor's project is not yet over, with a *Year Zero*-related HBO mini-series in the pipeline. When we make a credit card purchase, vote, tweet, update our status, upload our images, blog, watch TV, express an opinion, put on a t-shirt, visit the toilet in a club, what ARG are we playing? What web-strands are we causing to vibrate?

For Fisher, *Star Wars* marks the sea change because it was precisely 'designed as a hyper-commodity; not so much a film as a fictional system'. Commodification revolves here around 'hype', which is something more abstract than objects. 'Hype vorticism' anticipates discussions around the phenomenon media theorists currently call 'transmediality'. In the trans-medial, the sense of the hermeneutic experience of an original text begins to wither as we become immersed in labyrinthine, fabulatory systems, as meaning becomes operational, a doing with from within – the 'hype system' as world, as ontology, not representation – rather than a matter of interpretation from some point of exteriority. Increasingly, the experience of consumption is one of finding ourselves inside these systems rather than accessing a text from outside. Transmedial experience demands pattern-recognizing, puzzle-solving perpetual learners, cease-lessly intuiting the underlying algorithms. This gaming paradigm is, in sociologist Scott Lash's terms, a regime of post-hegemonic, ontological power. In Deleuze's terms, it is the cramped space of control-modulation. In Nolan's terms, it is the space of inception. It is Cloud space, the virtual enclosed.

The Cloud is SF Capital's most adventurous ARG hype system. If the Cloud suggests overt and transcendental religious connotations, if it promises a 'sacred canopy', this is deceptive. The control we're subject to is no longer hegemonic or transcendental, but rather ontological and immanent. Where Leadbeater conceives of the relations of the digital cloud 'hanging above us', we say, with Deleuze, they are rather 'within the very tissue of the assemblages they produce'.[39] The Cloud Thing is not a sacred canopy, it is intensive, inserting itself within life's tissue. Hence, its intransigence, its cramping of the space and time needed for resistance. It's going to be difficult to shift.

## Have Real Faith

In actuality then, despite Leadbeater's aims, capitalism has already re-defined itself here in the present, its appearance growing ever more indistinct as it further integrates difference. The ghost of Winstanley is given flesh in the science fictional laboratories of contemporary capital and promptly let loose as bewitching weapon of mesmeric force. Consider, for example, the glowing foreword to the 'Cloud Culture' report, written by then Foreign Secretary David Miliband. Leadbeater has long advocated flexible, network-based work, frequently championing the 'knowledge-based economy', and Miliband is very much in step with him here – no doubt flying the flag for Britain's cultural or creative 'industries', he tellingly states that 'the politics of *cloud culture* is politics of the people, by the people.'[40] This comment raises the spectre of two of Winstanley's contemporaries: the Hobbesian 'people' in opposition to a Spinozan 'multitude'.

As Paolo Virno points out, the *multitude* is typically understood as 'the form of social and political existence for the many, seen as being many ... a plurality which does not converge into a synthetic unity' and thus, crucially, counters the imposed unity of the state.[41] Historically, this concept has lost out to the notion of 'people', in which the many become condensed into the One and subject to the hegemonic authority of sovereign power, the state as Leviathan. Virno makes it clear that, for Hobbes, these two notions are in absolute conflict, it's all or nothing: 'if there are people, there is no multitude; if there is a multitude, there are no people.'[42] With the arrival of the cloud, this either/or dualism collapses, the multitude here redefining the One and vice versa, two forms of multiplicity operating as an assemblage but, importantly, not in the liberating fashion outlined by Virno. The cloud forms a disjunctive synthesis, or *controllable unity of the many*, based on a fundamental deceit: we see ourselves as multitude, we use the language and wear the clothes of multitude, indeed the continual productive success of the Cloud requires us to react in the inventive and creative manner that *defines* the multitude, but at the same time the Cloud operates as management and control through unifying structure. Rather than shock and awe, this is a counterinsurgency. It is the cooptation of the multitude *as multitude*, as distributed network of individuals; the unity described no longer takes the state or sovereign form, it exerts its power precisely *through the multitude*. Consequently, the power of cloud capital lies in the virtuality of the multitude itself, in its potential.

So why a *cloud*? Why something that is 'hanging above us'?[43] As if in response to the nihilism of digitality, the Cloud represents a curious techno-messianism, the rationalization of the transcendent into an anomalous science *of* faith and science *as* faith. Perhaps like any faith, cloud capitalism operates on the level of constructed plausibility, but further on a 'scientificism' – actually nothing more than a science-fictional expression of the fantastic – where shifts to the rules of the game are accepted and embraced because of appearance: 'not on the language of science, nor on the command of that language, but on the *appearance* of that command.'[44] Faith, here, is an ontological virus that works by persuasion and through the simulation of systemic authority, infecting with consensus. And, as the systematization of this viral faith coagulates in the infected assemblage of capital-security-control, the cloud must be understood as the apotheosis of 'faith-based' politics.

Faith-based politics is politics at gut level. Let's consider an example from the Presidency of George W. Bush, a tenure in the world's highest office that still continues to shape the present and is far from ready to be consigned to history. The 2004 Presidential election – won, to global consternation, by the incumbent Bush with an increased majority – was fought in hostile fashion on both sides, campaigning focused around the ongoing wars in Iraq and Afghanistan. In the run-up to the election, *The New York Times* published an article in which the journalist Ron Suskind detailed a conversation he'd had with an anonymous senior aide to Bush.[45] Complaining about a previous article Suskind had written, which had been critical of White House staff, the senior aide expressed his irritation:

> The aide said that guys like me were 'in what we call the reality-based community,' which he defined as people who 'believe that solutions emerge from your judicious study of discernible reality.' I nodded and murmured something about enlightenment principles and empiricism. He cut me off. 'That's not the way the world really works anymore,' he continued. 'We're an empire now, and when we act, we create our own reality. And while you're studying that reality – judiciously, as you will – we'll act again, creating other new realities, which you can study too, and that's how things will sort out. We're history's actors ... and you, all of you, will be left to just study what we do.'[46]

To have done with judgement. The actors act and, in doing so, reality is reborn, whilst all the critics must just stand back and see this creature's tail zip by. This, for Suskind is faith-based politics: the absolute faith in *will* (and in this case, the will of the president) rendering actual evidence secondary, even unnecessary.[47] It's curious, but that there is *no alternative* to this reality as defined by systemic authority is something we simultaneously accept as specious and yet consent to. SF realism, perhaps. Not, then, an idealised or abstract science but, as China Miéville puts it, 'capitalist science's bullshit about itself.'[48] The Cloud subjects faith-based politics to a process of rationalization, rationalizing faith itself as part of an overall will to truth. The truth, *reality*, becomes created through a seemingly totalizing assemblage from which there appears to be no outside. The 'open' nature of the cloud commons thus includes and encloses 'all' truths, all virtuals, in order that its resultant truth-assemblage is one that enables constant modulation, revision and renewal. Actual evidence, then, becomes irrelevant – there are no outside possibilities. As the aide says, *when we act, we create our own reality*. The rationalization of faith into something palpably manipulable and the corresponding *re*actions to that faith enable an absolute control of the truth, an absolute control of reality.

Rationalization is a vital component of a contemporary politics that accelerates beyond the clumsy necessities of pure ideology and, rather, towards systems of maintenance, management and administration.[49] Cloud culture, through its 'totalizing' structure, effects a disjunctive synthesis of faith-based doctrine and science-fictional rationality, or SF realism, that comprises a post-political politics of faith.[50] The 'reality-based community' and the 'faith-based community' comprise this disjunctive synthesis to equal degree; there becomes an absolute faith in a reality that is simultaneously accepted as unreal, the only reality being the reality of faith itself. A faith, then, in the *will*, in a 'process' and not a 'thing'. This is truth not as transcendent, Orwellian 'Ministry of Truth' but formed through and *as* the commons: we 'create and perceive our world simultaneously', Cobb tells Ariadne in *Inception*. There is no pre-existing or objective 'reality' in cloud culture, instead a network of 'always-on' nodal points work to capture difference, augmenting data within an autopoietic system. Invention drives capital as process, its control of difference ensures a state of security is maintained. Truth, reality in this sense, is in a state of constant creation, existing as the immeasurable assemblage of those multiple truths comprising the network-of-networks. As such, while the 'truth' of cloud culture is defined in the relational structure of the commons, it's clear that it isn't going on 'above us' as Leadbeater's offhand remark implies, but rather within the assemblage itself, within a virtual, now enclosed commons, a will to truth constituted and constructed through the multitude. With an operating philosophy of difference, the Cloud collapses transcendent values into flexible, manipulable immanence.

Winstanley himself sought to collapse transcendent values into the vitalism of the everyday, proposing the presence of 'heaven' within *this* world and God's immanence within all of 'material creation'. A God *as* earth in opposition to the Hobbesian sovereign God *on* earth. Winstanley wrote that a traditional Christian who 'thinks God is in the heavens above the skies, and so prays to that God which he imagines to be there and everywhere ... worships his own imagination ... '[51] Yet, in cloud culture, in which we also witness a collapse of transcendent values, that rationalized immanent imagination, that rationalized potential, is precisely the source of our faith; we worship the virtual within the actual. A post-political faith: 'if God is everywhere, if matter is God, then there can be no difference between the sacred and the secular: pantheism leads to secularism.'[52] If, with the capture of invention-power, the virtual becomes reduced to 'everywhere', if there is no virtual outside the enclosed 'totality' of the Cloud, if there is nothing capable of permanently escaping a rational lock-down and definition, then there is equally no difference in difference. We thus enter a state of total nihilism, the truly revolutionary power of the virtual denied, banned. While the resurrection of Winstanley undoubtedly highlights the urgent need for radical thought, his canonization by contemporary capital, even if conducted super-ficially, serves to simultaneously nullify that radicalism. We must recognize the dazzling appropriation of a commons-aesthetic – the *image* of Winstanley becomes exactly that, a holographic Dorian Gray capitalism that seeks to preserve a stolen youth, to inculcate an intensive and energetic vitalism which, in actuality, and as Wilde put it, is 'withered, wrinkled, and loathsome of visage.'

While Winstanley's ghost has been domesticated, communism itself has been imitated, consumed and adopted by capitalism. To put it in Virno's terms, post-Fordism is the 'communism of capital'. Virno reads the capitalist response to the 'defeated revolution' of the 1960s and 70s as an 'insidious and terrible interpretation' of communist objectives which, as suggested, depends upon harnessing the invention-power of the multitude.[53] Extending Klein's 'shock doctrine', we could perhaps even see communism itself (reduced, in its post-1989 state of disoriented crisis, to a spectre-like theory looking only to the past) as that which became subject to enclosure, to seizure. In this respect, the Cloud is the current state of a long-term project of rationalization that eliminates the possibility of the return of an 'outside' communism, an altercommunism. Cloud capitalism expresses the total capture of the multitude through the very language of communism, albeit, this language is a ventriloquist distortion, words are twisted: the dissolution of 'the state' and the abolition of 'work' become means of instituting control rather than delivering freedom. Collaborative, networked-based work, for example, becomes mediated by algorithm, predicated on systems of code, a staged engagement. As a result, and despite Hardt and Negri's early conviction that 'the commons is the incarnation, the production, and the liberation of the multitude,'[54] the commons should now be more accurately aligned with a communism of capital. Cloud commons is the banalization of the radical, 'digging' through the prism of nihilism. It is a capture of heretic energies. The commons becomes what Nietzsche called the 'social straitjacket', the place where we are '*made* truly predictable'[55] and yet this cloud commons is equally where *we make ourselves* predictable.

We can say, then, that the *potential* represented by invention-power reveals the immanent *value in the virtual*, in that which is real but not yet actual. Immanent virtuality is the realm where potential and domination meet, the contested site of power-over and power-to, the escape of imagination and creativity and the value inherent in their capture. It's therefore necessary to further consider the enclosure of the cloud commons as part of a programme to capture and secure the virtual.

Giorgio Agamben's revival of the notion of the 'state of exception' is interesting in this context; he describes a state of exception as resulting from measures taken in the event of a political crisis or emergency. These measures are in themselves paradoxical: the law of the state of exception is the suspension of law itself. A similar paradigm of security is fundamental to cloud culture but, crucially, this state of exception is *ontological* rather than exerted by hegemonic or sovereign power. When the experience of the everyday is mediated by the control of algorithm, protocol and the technological nonconscious, our choices, our *action*, becomes subject to this same 'exception'. As we hope to make clear, algorithmic control enables the *pre-emption* of action in quantifiable terms. In the open cloud commons, we do not find ourselves banned or excluded from the network society but we are rather banned from the fullness of the virtual(s), as they become locked down and archived. The collapse of the virtual into the actual serves as a way of identifying and securing the multiplicity of immanent potentialities – as a result, this process must be further understood as the selective *exception of the virtual*. The obvious outcome of such a strategy is that certain virtuals become 'unnameable and unclassifiable', indeed in the 'total' network-of-networks they become *unimaginable*, beyond conception. That not 'inside' the total archive cannot exist, even in potential form. The exception of the virtual is thus a strategy of depoliticization, the continual actualization of all potential implying that there is nothing beyond the system of which we are a part, the only questions able to be asked are those to which we already know the answer. As ontological control, the state of exception in cloud culture is thus further definition of modulative enclosure.

## 'Another Deeper Cave'

Dorian Gray capitalism, we've said. And Usher capitalism, too. Edgar Allan Poe's innovation in gothic horror, with 'The Fall of the House of Usher', was the house become monster. Poe's rewiring of the gothic teratologized the world in which we live, shifting from the haunted house to the haunting house. As the Cloud prepares for its disappearance into the nonconscious, we encounter an increasingly haunting world, a world in which nature, life, the body, politics are ghost-written, ghost-programmed. The Cloud is the last name of the ghost in the world-machine before the world becomes itself uncanny. Power is on the point of becoming ontological-hauntological.

Perhaps our response might take the form of 'escape' further and deeper into the cramped haunt of the Cloud, to claim it by ruse, by what Deleuze calls 'the powers of the false', games with games. It's as if we imagined a Trojan horse within a Trojan horse, matching and surpassing inception with fabulatory deception. In reference to Plato's simile of the cave – in which we are shackled to mere shadowplay, oblivious to the procession of the real under the rays of the sun outside – Nietzsche writes in *Beyond Good and Evil*, under no illusion that the procession is any more real than the shadows, that behind every cave, there is 'another deeper cave – a more comprehensive, stranger, richer world beyond the surface, an abysmally deep ground behind every ground, under every attempt to furnish "grounds."'[56]

Working through the post-political nihilism of the Cloud means seizing this abysmal hope and unleashing the contagious powers of the false.

Further, combat with cloud capitalism most certainly means apprehending it in its temporal dimension. Marx, as Fisher tells it, sought judgement upon capitalism in some near future in which its fiction, its lie – the speculative abstraction of value – would be reversed into truth, pure 'fleeting, virtual and abstract' capital 'cashed out' and back into concrete labor-time, returned to use value which is something we can get our heads and hands around (and at which point, as Fisher notes, all fictions are supposed to be unmasked). However, in 'human-all-too-humanist' mode, Marx didn't grasp the fictionality and virtuality of value *tout court*, didn't grasp Nietzsche's point about the world-making powers of the false, of the mask. On this point, perhaps, he didn't grasp capital itself (although, in our next chapter we will suggest Marx is capable of working with fiction in more sophisticated ways than Fisher suggests). This leads his thought of revolution into its confounding by hauntology, as observed by Derrida. Marx is caught up with ghosts, caught up in the paradoxes of his own 'retrospeculative fiction', unable to satisfactorily actualize the present in terms of either his fiction of the future or fiction of the past. But capital has no such worries about the fictionality of speculation. It simply works.

# Chapter 2

# Parasite Regime

*Protocol is an affective, aesthetic force that has control over "life itself". This is the key to thinking of protocol as power.*
Alexander Galloway

*We are certainly within something bestial ... Our host? I don't know. But I do know that we are within. And that it's dark in there.*
Michel Serres

Here we take what may appear to be a digression but is rather an effort to negotiate the disjunctive synthesis Cloud discourse comprises: between stuporous ineffability on one side and a fanatically detailed embrace of techno-banality on the other, the twin rhetorics of sprawling empty endorsement and schematic cataloguing of specification. To plot this course we follow the more recent efforts of some researchers to consider life after the exodus from screen-based static desktops – that is, the integration of virtuality and actuality effected by ubiquitous media – as a 'third age' of computing, even a 'third-order' cybernetics. In this mixed, augmented and increasingly complex reality, we find ourselves in dynamic relation with multiple time/spaces, dipping in and out of pervasive data streams, adapting to subtle systemic shifts. In short, with the coming of the Cloud, we find ourselves part of an affective media ecology and it's to this we now turn our attention.

## Artful Monster

Capital is the artful monster. It makes a semblance of life, a real abstraction. It is the arch-manipulator of perception. Let us follow Brian Massumi to try to clarify this thought.[57] Perception is a lived and vital encounter. It is dynamic, relational. Something happens, something unfolds. It is not really about perceiving objects as such, fixed and self-identical, but rather objects as actual embodiments of potential. We perceive the virtuality and processuality of the object, its self-differing – past and future held in the present – as a kind of halo or fringe of ripples or vibrations. And this movement in and of the object moves us, too, tugs us out of ourselves and our vibrations merge, becoming together. For Massumi, this is perception's 'vitality effect'.[58]

Ordinarily, we push the eventful nature of perception and the accompanying 'vitality effect' into the background – in perceiving, in the usual run of things, we don't want to feel alive, necessarily, we just want to achieve something, we are wrapped up in instrumental action and just want to put the object to use. Here, then, it is important for us to relate to objects as fixed, ready for use and interaction, apprehended in such a way as to foreground action and reaction.

In art, however, we are involved in the creation of artifacts which are precisely dedicated to stepping aside from ordinary interactions with objects, dedicated to capturing the dynamic relationality of perception in suspension. Francis Bacon, recall, claimed that the true function of art is to 'unlock the valves of feeling', to return the viewer to life, to make us feel more intensely alive and vital.[59] Art makes a 'semblance' of life, which in Massumi's terms, means that in it perception is doubled and becomes self-aware – this doubling is what he calls 'thinking-feeling'.[60] That vitality and virtuality in perception which is ordinarily only implicit, because it obstructs our everyday business-like interactions with objects, becomes explicit, is foregrounded. Art prompts us to think-feel what is happening, to affectively seize our encounter with the world as it dynamically unfolds.

The semblance of life is a form of appearance, a real

abstraction, which suspends/captures the virtual in the actual. Life's potential is gripped immanently. Now, crucially, as Massumi says, semblances 'lend themselves to regimes of power' as much as 'powers of resistance'.[61] Rather than the artwork, consider the commodity. The commodity is a semblance of the life it abstracts. The halo or ripple-fringe of an object's virtuality, under capitalism, becomes the uncanny aura-animation of the commodity fetish. If, in art, the semblance makes the virtual appear in order to make us think-feel alive, Capital captures the semblance to put the virtual to work. Under capitalism, of course, the production of semblances is captured, life abstracted, in order to extract surplus value. It is an 'institutionalization' of potential which gives it over to government by principles of utility and profitability. It is a fundamentally exploitative process, and it is imperative for capitalism that all visible traces of it, insofar as this is possible, must be made to vanish. Capitalism, then, is a self-occulting art form, an aestheticization of the world which masquerades as calculation, which foists upon us the interactive game in place of the eventful experience.

Value, the abstraction of life, of living labor, appears to us in the semblance-form of the commodity. However, Capital has been unable to completely abstract life. Life has preserved an autonomous aspect, an excess that refuses fixture into the economic operations of the capitalist machine. Nevertheless, Capital is compelled to attempt subsumption of this excess, to capture brains and bodies, capture the commons, reach into our soft tissue in furtherance of its extraction of value through extending its operations into the social. The late seventies saw the fulmination of, as Tiqqun put it, 'an entire world of counter-subjectivities', refusing the shackles of production and consumption, throwing into doubt even subjectivity itself. In response, Capital retooled itself: '*They* set up, then left in place, an entire complex machine to neutralize all that carries intense charge. A machine that defuses all that might explode.'[62] The world Rights itself, by which we mean that Capital takes the challenge as a signal to set in motion its own recomposition, responding to the life of resistance with its own experimental leaps. This occurred, in the seventies, specifically through the process aimed at the digital capture of life by means of what the Italian Autonomists named 'cybernetic command'. This is akin to what Massumi calls the gaming paradigm, and it also informs what Alexander Galloway has identified as the power of protocol.

We argue that, precarious and vulnerable in such experimental forays, Capital willingly puts itself at risk. In fact, Capital's exploitation of sources of its own jeopardy is key to its cybernetic experimentality. The principle of 'constructive instability' is pertinent here. Deliberately defective construction, courting failure, has long been recognized by engineers as potentially immensely productive. Constructive instability refers to the engineering of processes of collapse in an artefact which can be turned to good use. Elsaesser gives the example of the prototype American fighter plane, the X-29, the wings of which swept forward to exploit certain opportunities for enhanced manoeuvrability, changing course in allowing itself to fall through the air rather than frittering away energy maintaining a stable path. In conventional aerodynamic terms this was foolhardy, and a computer system had ceaselessly to check and make adjustments in order to prevent disaster: 'If this system were to fail for even one-quarter of a second, the X-29 would have tumbled out of control'.[63] For Elsaesser, constructive instability is a kind of programmed 'parapraxis' (the Freudian slip), a fostering and milking of slips, spillages, falls and teeterings. The principle applies also to the incursion of engineering and programming into life, drawing on and harnessing visceral and affective mutability, the ultimately uncontrollable emergence and emergency of life processes. On the back of all this, Capital writes the manual for extracting value from pathology.

Capital's parapraxical essays into the common viscera are already prefigured in Marx. The situation Marx sets out in *Capital* is precursor to both life's yoking by cybernetic command and the digital engineering of artificial life. With the emergence of value, Marx shows, on the one hand, life as subject to 'congealing' and, on the other hand, material objects as prone to springing into life. Life's flux slows, pools and gels in the form of the commodity-thing, while, dialectically, matter is vitalized, fetishistically animated when we mistake the form of appearance for what is really 'inside'. Capital constitutes a kind of intelligence which occults its own operations, artfully naturalizing the mystery of value and taking on vital form as 'second nature'. The construction of second nature (or even, as some commentators have suggested, third nature) is a process of aestheticization. In *Capital*, Marx, as Galloway suggests, '*aestheticizes capitalism* ... turns capitalism into media'. In doing so, Marx offers the Rosetta stone of capitalism, the codex that enables decipherment of the 'social hieroglyph', revealing 'how modern life is an aesthetic space through and through'.[64]

Anna Kornbluh extends this thought considerably, arguing that it was crucial for Marx that he achieved a stylistic hold on what it is about capitalism that is not conducive to assimilation in scientific or referential discourse. In the poetic register which flickers on and off in *Capital*, commodities address one another as persons, demonstrating their fluency in a bizarre new language. The text *personifies* the power of transformation that is valorization: 'When value is conjured as spiritual abstraction that authorizes exchange, the spirit transforms material bodies; personification discloses this spiritualization of the commodity body'.[65] Just so in *Capital* – Marx's great 'novel' – as in the modern world; all human persons are *mere* personifications, or 'masks', of 'the subject in this world', modernity's true protagonist, Capital (hence *Capital*, the title, stands as a proper name just as does, say, *Oliver Twist* for Dickens). The artifice Marx exploits in his theory-fiction alerts us to the artifice Capital foists upon the world in its own self-inception. It is 'the self-generating value which can perform its own valorization process'. This is a monstrous autopoiesis, the beast Capital hoisting itself by its bootstraps from the mire of matter, 'dripping from head to toe, from every pore, with blood and dirt'.[66]

Another tool Marx's poetics of capitalism employs, as Kornbluh shows, is the trope of *metaleptic substitution*. Metalepsy – literally, being seized by rampant alteration and exchange - is the promiscuous multiplication and combination of figures in order to elucidate a phenomenon. Marx proceeds by posing paradox, mounting figure upon figure, form of appearance upon form of appearance. Form is revealed as hiding equivalence and reversibility, this occulted mirroring exposed, for example, in Marx's insistence that 'since a commodity cannot be related to itself as equivalent, and therefore cannot make its own physical shape into the expression of its own value, it must be related to another commodity as equivalent, and therefore must make the physical shape of another commodity into its own value-form'.[67] Value is secured in a hall of mirrors, it isn't logically grounded, and Kornbluh's point is that its emergence can best be thought metaleptically, aesthetically. Things aren't really, naturally, commensurable, equal and equivalent. This is Capital's own theory-fiction or fabulation, an ungrounded 'as if', a 'makeshift for practical purposes', as Marx cites Aristotle.[68] A real abstraction, 'aesthetic form itself sublimates this impossibility; the value that is relationality is purely formal'.[69] Ungrounded, impossible, the murky contradictions at the heart of valorization, as Kornbluh concludes, are an abyss which Capital, like Marx's text, metaleptically hurls itself across in order to *retroactively* ground itself, its expansive power perfectly captured in this unfinalizable leaping and looping, deterritorializing/reterritorial-izing paradox-production. Capital/*Capital* – 'propulsive figurative machines' both – build their Penrose stairs, their dream architecture, evoke their ouroboric metaphysic: 'The looping motion of the narrative whose end is its own beginning, that can only find its beginning at the end, mimes the metaphysic of capital, its positing its own preconditions'.[70]

The ouroboric, or mirror, metaphysic of Capital hinges upon constructive instability, the calculated leap into the void (and, sometimes, the fall, as in the recent global financial crisis). Interestingly, Elsaesser sets out to explore how the principle works in terms of the internet by following a trail of social networking and other Web 2.0 user-generated content-based sites. He finds that the route generated – his search-term is, of course, 'collapse' – in interaction with the machine's sort-algorithms and tag-clouds gives rise to a narrative constantly on the brink of collapse, taking him, as if guided by an omniscient God, 'all around the world' on an epiphanic, rhizomatic magical mystery tour, but also, stupidly and entropically, 'nowhere at all', into chaos, 'the Hell of eternal in-difference and infinite repetition'.[71] A world is generated, semi-scripted by the machine insofar as it emerges from the programming architecture of the web, but also chaotic, random in terms of the human component, so that, overall, the emergent 'story-world' hangs together as a kind of 'structured contingency'. It oscillates between plenum and vacuum, or rather, in its onward, euphoric rush, it is a world metaleptically suspended over a void.

Semblance, parapraxis and metalepsy; here are some touch-stones for the analysis of aesthetic, affective capitalism, and, as we shall see, for the Cloud. Capitalism as machine for mediating life which, in doing so, strives to occult itself and vanish, is a self-regulating, self-made cybernetic art-monster. The informational-ization of life and the quantification and valorization of the human, has led us more and more to understand life as semblance, an aesthetic object. Thus, for example, biometrics 'considers living human bodies not in their immaterial essences, or souls, or what have you, but in terms of quantifiable, recordable, enumerable, and encodable characteristics. It considers life as an aesthetic object. It is the natural evolution of Marx's theory of second nature'.[72] Galloway draws on Marx because he wants to track the genealogy of life as medium, life as protocological. Life forms, whether organic or artificial, exist in 'any space where material forces are actively aestheticized', where matter is sculpted and 'vital agents are managed, organized, affected, and otherwise made aesthetically active'.[73] The forces regulating matter are the same as the protocological forces he describes in setting out, based upon Deleuze's thoughts on the 'monster' of Control, a reticular diagram of power.

## Error-Orror!

Power, as understood in Galloway's *Protocol*, is no longer bound up so much with visibility or the hegemony which centres on 'power over', or *potestas*. It now exists in a new form – 'power within', or *potentia*. Where sovereign power, turning on the single 'overseer', had its diagram of centralized control, and the disciplinary power that superseded it with its many watchmen had its diagram of decentralized control, power now exists immanently in terms of a diagram of distribution, a meshwork. The exigency determining this diagrammatic shift can be illustrated through the origins of the internet. The internet emerged principally within the Cold War context of the military imperative to overcome the threat of command centres being identified and taken out, thereby effectively crippling communication. Based on packet-switching technology in which messages are fragmented into data packets in order to make their way piecemeal, node to node, to their eventual destination and reassembly, the internet works rhizomatically, avoiding the need for central hubs. The communication and safe delivery of messages hinges upon protocols – technical standards managing the transfer of information. Protocols are formal, a matter not of message content but of the coding and wrapping of data packets for transportation. So far, so peer-to-peer. However, when we look closely at protocol, as Galloway urges, we actually discover two machines working together. The first machine – the rhizomatic one, as described – operates through the partner protocols of Transfer Control Protocol/Internet Protocol (TCP/IP), a pairing which governs the meshwork-based communication of autonomous nodes. The second protocological machine is altogether more hierarchically oriented – 'arborescent', in Deleuze and Guattari's terminology – revolving, as it does, around the Domain Name System (DNS), which is the massive database of addresses resident in a relatively small number of root servers, indispensable for the correct routing of data packets to named places in the network. It is this protocological 'dialectic' that secures stable and efficient communication, clarity of message, accurate delivery and predictable outcome. The nested layers of protocol preserve the content of the communication, check constantly that the packets keep moving in the right direction, automatically re-sending in case of irregularity or failure.

Protocol is of a piece with Deleuze's notion of the modulatory power which defines control society. Control is assured through flow. Nomadism is co-opted. Flows are both loosed and sorted, channels opened and pre-emptively managed and regulated, guaranteeing the eradication of threat or instability through innumerable sanctions and prohibitions. The protocological network diagram is technological, but also social and political. It materializes a post-hegemonic power and logic, vitalist, aesthetic and affective, erasing the distinction between life and network, bodies and technology.

Technocapitalism may be driven by totalitarian aspirations, seeking to encompass the whole of life, but its dominion is not actually total. Once again, it renders itself vulnerable as it ventures into this risky territory of life. Some commentators have exhorted us to consider the fallibility of the technology, its susceptibility to viral attack, glitching and data loss, or simply crashing. For Wendy Chun, Deleuze's notion of the control society is too bleak, a paralysing fiction. It paranoiacally overestimates the efficacy of the machine: 'it unintentionally fulfils the aims of control by imaginatively ascribing to control power that it does not yet have and by erasing its failures'.[74] Similarly, Mark Nunes urges exploration of the implications of error in digital systems, and seeks to impress upon us the importance of error's duality. The etymological roots of error – the word comes from 'err', to wander or stray – suggest a liberating directionlessness and purposelessness, 'an opening, a virtuality, a *poesis*'.[75] In its first sense, 'error', he writes, 'as captured, predictable deviation *serves* order through feedback and systematic control'. However, in its second sense of erring, straying, it 'evades prediction, program, and protocol. In those moments, an interstitial gap opens, an outside *within* the logic of the system that threatens "the good" of the system itself'.[76] Nunes commends a poetics of error or noise, a quest for unpredicted, productive 'moments of slippage' in which the system, an 'all-actualizing' machine when functioning correctly, is cracked open to virtuality, against its intentions giving issue to lines of flight.[77] Drawing on Umberto Eco's argument that poetics exploits the potential generated in textual 'equivocation', as opposed to the actualizing imperative of communication which depends upon reducing potential, Nunes presents a case for an aesthetic politics-poetics of error and noise to guide experiments with digital media technologies.[78]

Here, error is on the side of the angels (or, from the perspective of the machine, the side of the demons – error as horror). It is on the side of the virtual, life's power of difference and the production of the new. Error might intimate a semblance in Massumi's sense. If, with Foucault and Deleuze, power's object is now life – biopower – then effective resistance must entail recognizing life's excess, facilitating its escape from, and antipathy to, power and to the territorializing tendency of diagrams. This means a strategy of immanent transcendence. In the grip of power, any access to the 'outside', to the hellmouth of the virtual, must be found precisely via protocol, freeing life up from the cramped enclosures in which we find it, rather than going directly against it.[79]

The problem here, though, as we see it, is that the best proponent of error-horror is in fact the system, the propulsive machine of techno-capitalist metalepsy itself. As both Marx and William Burroughs knew, total control is no control at all. The sinews of Capital's greatest strength are in its jeopardy, in its 'makeshift', its 'as if', its equivocation. The monster's hold is paradoxically based upon its precarity. Capital *itself* is a power of poiesis. Its own main line of investigation is aesthetic and affective, experimental and vitalist. Metaleptic, self-launching, Capital is, with Elsaesser, 'productive pathology'. It feeds and fuels itself at the very brink of collapse, uses the moment, vampirizes the slip, the state of emergency. Control is inseparable from structured contingency, constructive instability. The drive for totality is pursued precisely through performative error, the invitation to collapse. As Nigel Thrift comments, capitalism threads any promising scientific developments in the wild 'into its very fabric through a combination of rhetoric, experiment and intuition'.[80] Just so, it also tracks the exploits of those who resist it. Paranoia, *pace* Chun, is essential. Imagine a free space, and the artful monster is breathing down your neck, studying the experiment, exploiting it and selling it back to you almost instantaneously. Capitalism infiltrates to exfiltrate, knowingly patrolling the jungles in its interstices, just to see what happens. Capital's back is never turned. It is all front (in more ways than one). We underestimate it if we think it turns a blind eye to wanderings, a deaf ear to the racket of its own undoing. This is its grist – both cursed in gnashing of teeth and turned to profit.

## Cthulhu's Reign

Okay, maybe this goes too far. But we must not underestimate the hold Capital's spell has upon us, the grip of the 'infernal alternatives' it has fabricated.[81] The first alternative, which goes by the slogan, 'There Is No Alternative', is basically what Mark Fisher has described in terms of 'capitalist realism'.[82] It constitutes an 'atmosphere' in which any attempt to rock the boat and foment dissent, even merely contemplate some other form of life, is met with dismay, choked off by charges of irresponsibility: 'We're all in it together'. The second alternative is that we set ourselves, thus provoked, diametrically against this 'reality', fall back on denunciation or terror and appeal to some transcendent power which will rise up against capitalism. Both of these alternatives short-circuit politics. Both are forms of capitulation and impotence, becoming indistinct and together comprising our current nihilistic disjunctive synthesis. On the one hand, a passive, cocooning, numbed-down nihilism is nurtured within us that forsakes difference for the actual, turns its back on the outside power of life, on the virtual. On the other hand, we turn tail from the actual to embrace a radical, scorching nihilism, fantasizing a clean-break escape, a flight into the outside, into the sun.[83]

This play of realism and fantasy ultimately comprises a post-political zone of indistinction. There has to be a third, non-infernal alternative. It must be that we cleave to the tension between virtual and actual, hope for immanent transcendence from within this zone of indistinction. Denunciation is especially tempting. But it is not an effective way of challenging the power of abstraction that is Capital. Philippe Pignarre and Isabelle Stengers insist that we need an 'ethology' of capitalism, that is, we need to study its behaviors as if it were an animal: 'what we must construct, as a hypothesis, is a way to characterise the frightening capacity that this being has of escaping one's hold' and 'how it keeps a hold over us'.[84] First and foremost, it's crucial to see that there is no Master Plan, no blueprint, but rather a host of subtle experimental processes and captures in all of its parts: 'This great irresistible wave is actively, laboriously fabricated by a multitude of local actors'.[85] There have been a number of important recent responses to the creaturely, inhuman power of Capital which begin to suggest an ethological approach. Autonomist Marxism theorized a 'double helix' binding and incorporating the struggle of workers into ongoing capitalist reorganization. Worker revolt is sucked into and recuperated by the propulsive capitalist machine, and every twist of the spiral it must strive again to move fast enough to spin away from the stranglehold.[86] For their part, Hardt and Negri champion the multitude against Empire. It is the multitude that is the monster. They pitch its monstrous flesh, capable of carnivalesque mutation and creativity, of turning the world upside down, against Empire, while Empire, in its turn, strives to appropriate this monstrous power.[87]

Capital's responsiveness, its constant restructuring of its functioning to prevent any hold on it and to subsume any such attempt suggest a creature which is capable of taking any form, a centreless creature which resembles a rhizomatic structure, a distributed meshwork. If it were an animal, as Pignarre and Stengers already propose, Capital would be a cephalopod, an octopus or a squid.[88] Jaron Lanier rhapsodizes cephalopods' ability to morph. By his account of a video of *Octopus vulgaris*, an algae-covered rock is revealed as consisting largely of this beast which can transform its skin into a screen across which it, in effect, plays an animation which mimics algae: 'cephalopods are the strangest smart creatures on Earth. They offer the best standing example of how truly different intelligent extraterrestrials (if they exist) might be from us, and they taunt us with clues about potential futures for our own species ... By all rights, cephalopods should be running the show and we should be their pets'.[89] The notion of the mimic octopus or vampire squid as dominant power is nothing new. If the rise of Weird fiction is anything to go by, we have certainly entered into what China Miéville dubs the 'Tentacular Novum': 'The spread of the tentacle – a limb-type with no Gothic or traditional precedents ... from a situation of near total absence in Euro-American teratoculture up to the nineteenth century, to one of being the default monstrous appendage of today, signals the epochal shift to a Weird culture.'[90] The problematic ontology – teeming, uncontainable – of the weird creatures populating the pages and images in the work of H.P. Lovecraft, William Hope Hodgson, through to Stephen King's *The Mist*, Guillermo Del Toro's movie *Hellboy*, and Miéville's own novel, *Kraken*, is entirely of a piece with the metamorphic evolution of Capital: 'In quick and dirty caricature, with the advent of the neoliberal *There Is No Alternative*, the universe was an ineluctable, inhuman, implacable, Weird, place.'[91]

Capital, like Lovecraft's Cthulhu, rules through miniature iterations of itself, its spawn, the mindless 'minions' described by Pignarre and Stengers. Ray Brassier points out that we should resist the temptation to mystify Capital, treating it as if it really were 'an impersonal, wholly autonomous agent subsisting quite independently of the myriad of little human subjects who compose it'. It is not this 'superhuman' agent but rather an utterly banal but complex effect emergent from 'the myriads of micro-processes that compose it...'[92] This point is well taken. Nevertheless, approaches which cast their lot in with error, or defuse paranoia with reference to the banality of capitalism's enforcement, perhaps underestimate the intransigence of Capital. And so do, in a different way, Hardt and Negri, with their notion of the monstrosity of the multitude's flesh. Their message is that: 'We need to use the monstrous expressions of the multitude to challenge the mutations of artificial life transformed into commodities, the capitalist power to put up for sale the metamorphoses of nature, the new eugenics that support the ruling power.

The new world of monsters is where humanity has to grasp its future.'[93] Monstrous flesh as a figure for the creativity of the multitude – the creativity which Capital leeches off – does not give full weight to the pervasiveness of Capital. As Steven Shaviro notes, Capital precisely 'incites' monstrosity in order to channel and exploit it: 'Hardt and Negri write as if the creativity of the multitude came first, as if it were only at the last moment that capital stepped in, to appropriate this creativity and sell it in commodified form. But in fact, capital is always already there, always already monitoring and regulating everything that we do, even before the creative process begins.'[94] So Hardt and Negri are too precipitant. They have it the wrong way round in that once Capital, like Cthulhu, descends from the interstellar gulfs, everything changes. It erases its contingency. Again, this is the retroactive grounding of what is essentially ungrounded. It's *as if* it was always there; there never was, never is and never will be any alternative, any outside to its irresistible dominion, its dreaming.

It's Capital that is the monster, we who are the parasites. We are lodged within the cramped cavities of its body, the coils of its guts. It precedes us and is our experiential matrix: 'we are the parasites, not capital. We cannot experience this capital-body directly, and for itself; yet all our experiences are lodged within it, and can properly be regarded as its effects.'[95] Life is now thoroughly designed, engineered and programmed. Aestheticized, fabulated. This is the weird horror of technocapitalism, Capital as media, 'everting', folding and disappearing into life itself, becoming invisible as our nonconscious, algorithmic body.[96]

## To the Cloud

Speaking at the London School of Economics in 2010, Microsoft CEO Steve Ballmer cheerfully admitted his own inability to 'nail' a description of the Cloud. Despite the tumult of commentary, proclamation and excitement, the Cloud is revealed as *indescribable*. The Cloud is something that 'understands and brings knowledge' or, echoing Eric Schmidt, 'understands you and what you want,' getting 'smarter every day' – it is a power of definition, one which determines knowledge, truth and the ability to act.[97] Yet, even as consumers 'implicitly embrace' this anthropomorphic power, one which brings and ascribes value to the known, the Cloud remains an *unknown* force. It is an overdetermined, unutterable power of transformation, an escapee from 'the prison-house of the known' as Lovecraft had it. Infused within the fabric of the social itself, the Cloud Thing effects a mediated and banalized numinousness, a *full spectrum media*.

As we have suggested, labor is no longer premised on sedentarism – production and consumption have been thoroughly integrated and working life has become life-as-work. Media, here, is more than an overall technical system, more than a pluralization of 'medium'. Instead it is life itself, a state of conjoined relationality with the monstrous body of informational capital which becomes a pervasive environment for cognition, perception and affection. No longer a representational media*scape* we must instead consider this symbiotic relationship as a *media ecology* – in Matthew Fuller's words: 'the massive and dynamic interrelation of processes and objects, beings and things, patterns and matter,' one aligned to the collapse and convergence of diverse media into a single dynamic system 'in which any one part is always multiply connected, acting by virtue of those connections, and always variable, such that it can be regarded as a *pattern* rather than simply as an object.'[98] This patterning brings about the codification of the everyday as 'ambient' media, a background hum to which we are acclimatized and accustomed, in which we live and breathe, and into which 'digital natives' are born. For Ballmer, the Microsoft Kinect system (a games console operated through voice and bodily movement) represents the inauguration of this transparency of human-computer interface, a process of *naturalization*, or the 'smooth alignment between bios and techné' as Elsaesser has it, an evolution where the disappearance of the screen is surely the next step.[99] The Kinect is merely an early prototype for what is yet to come. So, in contrast to the 'digital grid' of Disney's zombie-franchise spectacle *Tron: Legacy*, this is a baroque ecology, an encompassing inside-outside. Here, according to Ballmer, for user-producers to be 'in control', there must be a 'smart' relation with the Cloud, one that necessitates a processing of 'me'.

In this Cloud ecology, bare life is entwined with the socio-political, the effect of which has material, biological consequences. Let's return briefly to the nature of power in the Cloud, and particularly 'biopower' as defined by Foucault. Biopower differs from the sovereign power over life and death in that it is not individualizing, not an 'anatamo-politics of the body' but rather a biopolitics of the species, of the human race.[100] The field of biopolitics is concerned with what Foucault calls 'aleatory events', namely phenomena which can unexpectedly lead to a decrease in production or efficiency, accidents or ill-health for example. The biopolitics of the species is therefore concerned with strategies of measurement like demographics, methods which enable the rate of birth, death and fertility to be considered in statistical terms.[101] Moves are then made to 'intervene at the level at which these general phenomena are determined, to intervene at the level of their generality', in other words to actively modify life expectancy, birth rates and mortality through the institution of 'regulatory mechanisms' in order to counter or compensate for 'variations within this aleatory field'.[102]

With the coming of the Cloud, Foucault's tentative distinction between two types of power operating through technologies of the body – firstly, the body as *organism* 'endowed with capabilities' and, secondly, more general 'biological processes' – can be reconsidered as much closer to each other on a continuum of power, if not as one and the same. In fact, biopower is that which is more than the individual biological, more even than the sum of physical life. While Foucault insists that any perceived dichotomy between the two conceptualisations of technologies of the body is unintended, what's crucial in the context of the Cloud is that the body 'individualized' is very much that which he describes as 'a new body, a multiple body, a body with so many heads that, while they might not be infinite in number, cannot necessarily be counted.'[103] This, despite Hardt and Negri's insistence on a 'living social flesh that is *not* a body,' is the body of the multitude.[104] The Cloud heralds a technologically 'smart' body, an intensified coalescence of a prosthetic, proximal body of nodal points. The complexities of the body, then, are what define this new media ecology.

Michel Serres proposes a parasitical relational system; for him the environment of the collective is an indescribable animalistic form. He points to a 'cascade of parasites', a matrix of one-way relations, 'where one eats the other and where the second cannot benefit at all from the first', single arrow linkage, then – power travels in one direction only.[105] This system of relations is one of guest and host, a 'nesting series of vampires'.[106] However, the Cloud as *ecology* is a more complex world than this model of cascades, one-way relational chains or 'stepladder' formations; while it too determines knowledge, it negates the application of an *order* or hierarchical structure. As Serres suggests, *the host is not prey* because 'he offers and continues to give' and, equally, its other is not predator but parasite.[107] This is a relation of mutual reliance. In the Cloud ecology, in fact, both capital and multitude take on roles as host *and* parasite: the networked body of the social, the multitude, feeds off the monstrous body of capital while it, in turn, is nourished by that very body of the collective. Serres says that we're within a beast-host, clutched in the inner darkness. Shaviro says much the same thing. We say rather that the Cloud body constitutes a mutual, ouroboric parasitism of capital and multitude. We are in the Cloud and the Cloud is in us. This, then, is a weird ecology of immersion-eversion, a symbiosis of mutual dependence, one in which the 'social flesh' of the multitude becomes indistinguishable from the body of capital. The milieu and the body are thus conflated, and what Foucault called 'the urban problem' – the effects on a population by a non-natural environment – is today, a Cloud problem.[108] As media ecology, the Cloud *is* biopower, informatic nature, or what, following Paul Edwards, we might call a 'green-world', but one that is *naturally* closed, one that we travel within but equally travels within us. If Deleuze and Guattari say that we become with the world, here is the darkside of that becoming.

In his account of the interdependence between the development of computing technology and the context of the Cold War, Edwards details the rise of 'closed-world' politics.[109] A closed-world is described as one in which power adopts the form of a *system*, through centralization, increasing integration – of existing, disparate practices and techniques, in addition to human-machine integration – and reliance on mathematically and cybernetically driven automation. Moreover, the closed-world represents the ideal and follows the 'intrinsic logic' of capitalism, driven towards a scenario of total integration, the eradication of barriers, the guarantee of 'open' and 'free' markets where capital can flow without constraint.[110] A combination, then, of computerized control based on complex analysis of integrated systems and the erasure of barriers between human and machine which enables that computing to become cyborg-like, operating and undertaking production in the manner of a rationalized 'mind' or 'brain'.

Edwards identifies what we used to call 'cyberspace' as a classic closed-world, one in which 'everything has become information and information is all that matters,' one where value is only found in data.[111] On the face of it, then, the Cloud appears to be a closed-world – it takes on the role of 'collective computer' or 'world wide computer' as Tim O'Reilly and Eric Schmidt have put it respectively; it fulfils what Tim Berners-Lee (inventor of the World Wide Web) considers the raison d'être of the network, namely 'to get out of the way, to not be seen', to become natural.[112] In the case of the most successful material commodity-technologies, a balance must be struck between high visibility (essential to a marketing process predicated on constant upgrading) and a ubiquity that leads to a certain invisibility, a disappearance like trees within a forest. This kind of strategic hiding or disappearance is historically evident in numerous modes of production where, as Galloway suggests, an apparatus would be produced to hide an apparatus, disparately evident in both the capitalist commodity form and Hollywood continuity editing.[113] With cloud computing the apparatus becomes naturalized, the nature of the virtual network disappears because it is wholly imbued and embedded within the fabric of the social, 'lost' amid the structures of the everyday; as with Shaviro's description of the body of capital, we 'can no more "see" it than a flea can see the dog within whose fur it is embedded.' The Cloud is just another taken-for-granted service, an 'ontologically invisible digital technology'.[114] And yet, there is nothing *neat* about these relations of body-brain-culture, it remains a parasitic ecology, defined by a necessary infection. Its power remains virtual, its capacities in *excess* of the sum of its parts, a 'live torrent in time of variegated and combinatorial energy and matter', symbiotic, impossible to disassemble into components.[115] Its continued existence is, however, predicated on this *excess*, either through its release in order to grow and *expand* the commons, or though its consumption, thereby maintaining control over a 'total' structure.

For our purposes, the closed-world as Edwards presents it would be too simplistic a reading of the Cloud. It remains a diagram of centralized power, a purified world where parasites have been eradicated – for hegemonic power to be effective,

Serres indicates, 'one must be heard, listened to: the message of order must pass through silence. There must be silence. The parasites must be chased.'[116] Having adapted his closed-world concept from origins in Shakespearean literary criticism, Edwards extends the notion further to suggest a world 'radically divided against itself,' defined and consumed by conflict, a world 'without frontiers or escape' that 'threatens to annihilate itself, to implode.'[117] This is a world defined by violence in the name of peace. While it's true that the *natural* state of the Cloud is one loaded with a multiplicity of threats, each with the potential to turn inward, this trace of radical excess is never wholly out of control in its ecology. In literary theory, the alternative to the enclosed, *artificially* constructed environment of the closed-world is, instead, a 'green-world', a place of escape and refuge from structures of power, 'an unbounded natural setting' where a protagonist can move 'in an uninhibited flow' and tap into 'magical, natural forces'.[118] While the protagonist of a closed-world drama embarks upon a lonely struggle against the Other, the green-world protagonist enters into a collective quest where complexity becomes transparent, Others transformed into 'mere others', domesticated.[119]

As an ecology permeated with and held together by biopower, the Cloud effects what Foucault called the optimization of 'life' and the maximization and extraction of forces, doing so through the institution of 'regulatory mechanisms' – a post-disciplinary systematization. However, as we have seen, the compensation for variations in the 'aleatory field' does not necessitate a homeostasis or equilibrium but rather a continuous and self-organised modulation that ensures 'regularization' is also productive. 'Magical' or 'natural' forces are thus captured in order to *extract* from life-as-event 'that which is not exhausted by the happening ...'[120] As Nietzsche tells us, the state of the world is one of disequilibrium, a state of becoming rather than something 'created'. Coursing through the technology of the Cloud is 'a monster of energy, without beginning, without end.'[121] Accordingly, any dichotomy between 'closed' and 'green' worlds is no longer tenable. Instead, the mode of power described as operating by means of a closed-world discourse has captured and appropriated that promised by the green-world. It's not just that capital has enclosed the unbound settings of the green-world (although, as we have seen with the commons, this is true) but capital itself no longer works to contain a 'closed' world in the same way: internalization is inadequate, even the notion of an 'inside' space in which integration occurs becomes invalid. Rather, there is an integration based on *relations of exteriority* – the limits of capitalism become immanent to it – power is decentralized and highly distributed, within the flows themselves, within the *body* (capital, social, individual). The Cloud is media as force of nature, a world of transformational processes where power diffuses amid uneasy assemblages – a 'strange ecology' indeed. Far from exterminated, the parasite is everywhere. Expansion, proliferation becomes fundamental: 'the absolute empire of relation.'[122] This host-parasite power, as Serres makes clear, is one of the voice, of sound, and of noise.

In his playful discussion of a fable of two rats feasting on the leftovers from a farmer's meal, only to be disturbed by the *noise* of the farmer outside the door, Serres suggests that 'the parasited one parasites the parasites,' the farmer 'jumps behind those who were eating behind his back and chases them.' We are again reminded of *Inception*'s Penrose stairs. Here, the host 'counterparasites' its guests, not by directly taking away the food from the rats but rather by *creating noise*, by scaring off the parasites and thus returning to a position of power within the overall system.[123] So, while the arrow of relations is not exclusively one-way, the 'power' experienced by the multitude is illusory, nothing more than a faint (or feint) arrow generated by *feedback* which serves to stimulate the production of further sustenance for capital. The Cloud ecology is a harness upon Nietzsche's world-as-monster-of-energy, an exploitation and abuse of excess, of surplus, applied in green-world expansion. The relation between capital and the multitude remains unequal; the network is asymmetrical, always in favour of capital-as-host, capital-as-parasite.

Crucially, however, in this symbiotic relationship between capital and the multitude, 'scaring off' the parasite with noise is no longer productive. Rather, noise becomes the means through which behavior comes under control. Instead, the host-parasite, the möbius, inculcates the multitude into a parasitical labor. Thus, the patterning of the everyday as 'ambient' is the inception of an affective *polyrhythmia*, a fluctuating data-saturation which refuses false distinctions between closed and open, social and biological, organic and nonorganic, between the multitude and the infrastructure of the everyday. It is in this respect that cloud computing seeks to disavow its own technological, material and empirical status: the giant server farms which provide the dynamically scalable and latent power resource remain, located in their various (secret) sites around the world, effectively invisible, irrelevant to our everyday connected relationality. Furthermore, our everyday actions are deemed to cast a lengthening 'information shadow' that is captured and logged; the structure of the everyday is pregnant with an information 'layer' – the system of parametric and algorithmic control to which we remain unaware – and social practices themselves are full of 'implied metadata', even and especially those interactions yet to take place.[124] What's more, the always-on archival ecology is awash in a dynamic *noise of data*, an immanent informational static, an *atmosphere* rather than a layer, something which 'gets into the individual' such that modulations and intensifications to its rhythm bring about physical and biological changes – a transmission of affect.[125] As suggested, in many ways this information shadow is nothing new (birth and death rates, systems of numerical identification, government records, even the

Domesday book), but the difference here remains palpable. An atmosphere of information – ambience rather than shadow – swells and mushrooms into an almost haptic static, the virtual increasingly a coagulum, increasingly actual.

Here, then, we are immunised to the general existence of noise. Less a linear or dialectical signal, less an on/off, presence/absence parasitism, the significance is the transition of noise to atmosphere, to oscillation on a continuum, a 'variable stability' that is equally an 'invariance by instabilities', a continual modulation of strength, intensity, affect.[126] Thus powerless to terminate the dynamic flow of informational energy, the multitude is exposed to recalibrations in the 'mechanics of the system', micro-adjustments which, induced in the technological unconscious, produce affective responses.

## Weird Ecology

Because it is before consciousness, before the fact of the 'person', affective life is beyond complete control: 'An affect is a non-conscious experience of intensity. It is a moment of unformed and unstructured potential'.[127] As an organism is stimulated, it prepares to act, generating responsive intensities as expressions of the stimulation's intensity. Affect is transmissible between bodies. Bodies resonate with the intensities they encounter, including those generated by media technologies: 'the power of many forms of media lies not so much in their ideological effects, but in their ability to create affective resonances independent of context or meaning'.[128] Affect's autonomy from individuated emotion, context and meaning means that it is not prone to any kind of direct control by the person. The key, rather, is what kinds of encounters we can organize, what events of affect we can solicit. Or, indeed, what kinds of encounters, events of affect, can be organized on our behalf by the smart-body in which we lodge.

In perception, we feel our aliveness. This can become self-aware, the thinking-feeling of what happens. But, as we have seen, it is normally not explicit. Especially in the 'gaming paradigm', the 'interactive situation', which is all about instrumental action, the compulsion to participate, to express oneself is prevalent. Massumi, recall, contrasts this with art – art is the creation of semblances, precisely concerned with suspending chains of action-reaction, producing a stalled moment in which potentiality becomes perceptible and we are returned to life. Where the aesthetic experience offered by the system, in what has come to be called the diagram of 'gamification', is part of a soft, affective tyranny, a radical aesthetic politics, in which art is formulated as a subversive 'exploratory politics of invention', would involve the interruption of the game situation with semblances. However, the gameworlds into which we are anticipatively engaged by capital are built to discourage such interruptive ructions.

As elements of capital's smart-body, we are exercised, our body keeps us on our toes. This is aesthetic, affective control under Cthulhu-Capital's reign. More than any specific affect, it cultivates readiness. It sets its sights on anticipation. The system operates on corporeal anticipation. Far from narcotizing subjects into dazed docility, it intoxicates, overloads and renders ecstatic, ultimately giving rise to a detritus of ill, wasted, burnt-out subjects.[129] This go-to intervention into the body's anticipative capacities, this affective enclosure, is what we have called inception – inception of the future, inception of a world. It constitutes Capital's experimental groping towards the full realization of post-hegemonic ontological power. We live the 'secular magic' of affective capitalism's 'worlding', modulatory enclosures, calculated yet natural-seeming gameworlds.[130] This dynamic incorporation of a world within ourselves is effected by a spell that mustn't be broken.

What we focus on, how we relate to objects, 'structures of anticipation', and so on, all of this is prone to intervention now. A premediation industry is emerging. This is an industrial 'worlding', a kind of dreamwork, a construction of gameworlds for us to affectively inhabit. Worlding constitutes what Nigel Thrift considers to be the contemporary 'engineering of active spaces'.[131] It's not about creating discrete 'fully-formed spaces' that we might enter, but a more processual, 'mediological' detailing of already existing spaces in everyday life. This aims to make the spaces resonate in particular ways to create certain kinds of affect-effect. It's a 'boosting' of space, providing tools for the creation of new spaces. Just as seventeenth century theatre acted as an earlier form of worlding, in which audiences 'filled in the space by using their own imagination', contemporary engineered spaces routinely engage active participation and 'infill'.

## The Affect-Drop

The Cloud ecology is a means of naturalising operational linkage by means of *affect*, something distinctly bodily and thus separate from emotion or feeling, a system whereby relations of exteriority are joined together in an affectively linked collective body. Affect is precisely non-conscious. It is that which is always prior to, or outside of consciousness, formlessly preceding thought. Affects, then, are prepersonal, autonomic bodily reactions representing the ability of the body to act. While the manipulation of 'feelings' or 'emotions' is well-established (think, for example, about the importance placed on confidence by economists and politicians), the movement of power into the realm of the *prepersonal*, namely the micro-space prior to the translation of affect into sensation and its subsequent social display, is a movement towards capturing the expression of potential. The background hum of atmospheric information ensures that the emergence of the 'new' – that brought into being by an *excess*, surpassing the sum of its networked parts – is *efficiently* managed. The Cloud institutes a systematic mobilization of affective rhythms in order to modulate and maintain *readiness*, to ensure a preparedness to act that is instantly translatable into productive non-conscious resource.

According to writer and Microsoft researcher Jaron Lanier, the Kinect represents the beginning of a shift towards 'somatic cognition'. Just as we use words in the process of conscious thought, somatic cognition *extends* the human body. Lanier cites the example of 'learning to improvise' on the piano: once a certain level of practice has been undertaken 'a moment comes when you notice that your hands have solved complicated puzzles of voice and harmony faster than your conscious mind can keep up. Fine basketball players, surgeons and pilots report similar moments.'[132] With the dissolution of the human-computer interface, the increasing efforts of techno-capital to invade, modulate and govern this realm, where the nonconscious biochemical state of the body determines the power to act or *react*, must be recognised as an intensification of biopolitical – or *microbiopolitical* – power.[133] Control of the rhythmic informational pulses of the Cloud ecology enacts the mobilization and engineering of affect, the nonconscious programming of the body. Improvisation, here, is largely illusory. In this, the Cloud follows technological developments over the last two centuries which have sought to reveal that which is imperceptible, to pry open the spaces of so-called biological 'microstates', colonizing the prepersonal. As Nigel Thrift describes it, scientific instruments (such as the microscope) redefined the body as 'a set of microgeographies' and photographic techniques exposed previously invisible or unremarkable bodily movements.[134] The latter is evident in the work of Eadweard Muybridge and Jules-Étienne Marey who, in the field of physiology, worked to find ways of revealing the 'unknowable instant' amid sequences of physical movement. Marey's 'chronophotography' enabled discrete moments to be captured, 'cutting into time, slicing it in such a way that it could become representable.'[135] In their representation of the performance of certain actions, and in conjunction with the science of statistics, Marey's images became a tool for increasing human efficiency, particularly in a factory setting, where the smooth and ordered combination of atomised 'instants' – previously imperceptible – maximised human-machine productivity. The example of chronophotography illustrates that bodily potentials can thus be statistically quantified.

Crucial here is the importance of bodily *anticipation*, exemplified by the discovery of the 'half-second delay'.[136] This delay – between action and cognition – has been biologically demonstrated: an action is set in motion *before* we 'decide' to perform it. To be specific, an action is set in motion by the body approximately 0.8 seconds before we have the conscious experience of that acting. Experiments conducted by psychological researcher Benjamin Libet suggest that physical stimulation is only felt if it lasts longer than half a second and that sensation, as Massumi puts it, 'is organized recursively before being linearized, before it is redirected outwardly to take part in a conscious chain of actions and reactions,' or in Libet's own words, sensation involves 'a backward referral in time'.[137] We therefore respond to intentions *after* they arise. In terms of 'readiness', then, consciousness or thought occurs after the bodily action itself – consciousness 'takes time to construct'. Readiness exists in the body before it moves into the realm of conscious thought. Thrift defines this scientific stretching, epistemological widening and general intensification of the perceptible as a 'constantly moving *pre-conscious frontier*,' an exposure of the 'fleeting space of time' in which the body demonstrates anticipation, improvisation and intuition.[138] The expansion of power into this realm is, then, an 'inception', introducing an affect at the pre-personal level in order to nonconsciously generate personal feelings and, crucially, performative displays of social emotion. As the pre-cognitive components of subjectivity become mobilized, the Spinozan body-mind becomes 'the scene of the crime.'[139] The propensity to trust system-constructed truth, to have confidence in its protocological 'guidance', and to be fearful of future instability or aleatory events can all be calibrated in this state of readiness.

In the intensive-attention economy, in a state of always-on, readiness must be real-time, a *vigilant* state of alert and heightened awareness to quantum fluctuations in the affective rhythms of the Cloud ecology. There is no longer any need to 'check' messages, to 'search' for updates, rather, in a state of anticipatory preparedness, life becomes a multiplicity of quantum-responses to pre-conscious modulation. Here we can recall Burroughs's labelling of what we accept as 'reality' as nothing more than a constant scanning pattern.[140] The affective atmosphere of the Cloud is subject to change, but we unknowingly change with it. This 'reflex impulse' favours instantaneity, speed, over precision or accuracy, the concern is with continuation rather than progression. Again, this is a logic of the videogame, in which response and reflex become integral to the prolongation of the gaming experience, a maintenance that also demands 'power-ups', affective-boosts which serve to ensure a fluctuating normalisation. This conception of the Cloud as ludic-ecology, of life as gameworld, is, however, one with no 'escape' key. We can also think of readiness and response immediacy as an overall ontology of programmed habit to which we become algorithmically accustomed – patterning, in this sense, is a series of dynamic routines and sub-routines for life, each subject to quantum change. Here we return to Foucault's notion of the 'optimization' of life through regulatory mechanisms and mutable IF ... THEN responses. Hardt and Negri insist that habits, being shared and social, constitute 'the common' in *living practice*, that habits are themselves 'the site of creation and innovation.'[141] But rather than 'creating' a nature 'that serves as the basis of life,' habit as scanning pattern becomes a productive addiction, we become dependent on practices which maintain affective rhythms, those vital to our understanding of the world.

Moreover, under the control of protocol and algorithm life is re-established as a *performance*. The Cloud ecology is the affective environment in which this performance takes place, in the 'execution' or 'operation' of life, we collaborate in the mainte-nance of an overall consensus of contentment, a conservation of well-being and satisfaction (how do you rate your experience?) preserved via systems of interpersonal communicative-enter-tainment, through which we can deemed to have gained value from life. The translation of this stable affective continuum into emotional reactions is a key 'index of credibility' as Thrift puts it, a state of legitimacy increasingly demanded not just from public figures but from encounters in the everyday that demand the communication of emotional validity: commitment, confidence, belief. Life in the Cloud becomes a strategy of method acting, becomes artificial.

The incursion into the preconscious thus reveals the Cloud as operating with a microbiopolitical Manifest Destiny, staking a claim at this pried open frontier, mapping and surveying a new realm, moving ever deeper. It's here at the pre-conscious frontier that the affective power of informatic-ambience pulses with a collective beat. Imagine, if you will, a nightclub packed with Saturday night revellers. The kind of modulation in question, the building up of a state of preparedness, a readying for action, is familiar to those squeezed onto the dance floor. From his booth, the DJ effects a similar power over the sweating, stroboscopic body of clubbers: a throbbing rhythm synchronizes the multitude, individuals move together in time, the hum of the body an attestation to a life oscillating through it, moving between a rhythmic near-homeostasis and a rush of intensity. As rhythm is fine tuned, intensified, the body is ready, anticipating the future moment and thus shaping it. And then, *the drop*: an affective accent of non-conscious intensity that surges through the body.

To be nonconscious, to be lost amidst these waves of collective sensory energy, is also to take flight from the 'prison-house of the known', the descriptive labels of sensational, conscious experience. And yet, this is merely a loss of active determination, a functional integration of relations, and far from an escape. Tuned in to the affective frequencies of the Cloud, we receive transmissions of a resonance that moves through the symbiotic host-parasite body, through the body of capital, amid the hetero-geneous body of the multitude. Hence, the DJ's booth is immanent to the body, not external to it, the point at which social and biological rhythms coalesce – the Cloud ecology undulates to affective-algorithms, a 'soft machine' for the engineering of affect. So, the body is drawn into harmony with an ecology of media, falling in step with the binary-beat of ubiquitous infor-mation, a meta-stable environment in which the next pulse of the rhythm is performatively anticipated by the body, while all the time subject to micro changes.

Looking back at the dance floor, we can now see that the nightclub multitude are actually performing an undetectable choreography, one that's subject to a constant quantum modulation, a perpetual amendment to the routine, and thus remains imperceptible. Affects are 'grammatized', bodily gestures become discrete 'moves', quantum-abstractions from a continuum to permit 'automatic' reproduction and repetition.[142] As Steve Goodman suggests, being 'always-on', a node in an *open* network, means that the body is 'exposed to informational and affective contagion'.[143] Viral informatic-affect spreads from the body of capital through the multitude, mutating and trans-forming as it propagates; this circulation of affect is productive in itself, adding value to living, dynamic *trends*. Readiness is therefore also a condition in which production is conducted in anticipation of infection and a constant mutation into new states. In this respect, while waves of viral mutation continuously flow through the collective body of our nightclub dancers, in their weird take on Busby Berkeley they are disjunctively synchronised – to the extent that they are, uniquely, leaning or inclined in the same direction: toward the future. As we will see, always-on is also *always-already*. In the Cloud, production is always-already parasited; the creation of the new is followed by its immediate banalization. The 'unexpected' or 'improbable' is dragged out to a desert cemetery and preemptively buried, a Tarantino-style Texas funeral, 'where entropy rots matter away'.[144]

The Cloud ecology is thus a numinous and dynamic *pattern for life* where always-on cognitive labor is subject to preconscious control: radical rhythms, pacifying patterns, the amplification and adjustment of the collective body. An ecology is, of course, polyrhythmic and made up of a multiplicity of patterns – personal, social, fictional and real. The Cloud effects the diagrammatic association of these discordant movements into a system where Lefebvre's notions of isorhythmia (the living body comprised of an equality of associated rhythms) and arrhythmia (a 'pathological desynchronisation' that threatens the body) are disjunctively synthesised, the modulation between dynamic states serving to *engineer* affect.[145] Rather than a constructed control of actions, this is a calibration of predisposition, of the tendency to act. The Cloud therefore operates at a level beyond passive 'training' of the body to also induce a controlled affective shudder or jolt, a radical reset that staves off inefficiency, the deterioration of resonance. Waves continue to pulse ... a state of readiness also means never-at-rest.

## Bleeding the Future

*Where do you want to go today?* asked Microsoft with their ubiquitous branding slogan of the late twentieth century, the suggestion being that whatever our answer, however wild our dreams, it would *all* be perfectly achievable with the combination of network power and the right software. Of course, Microsoft answer the question for us: *To the Cloud.* Ballard proposed that the twentieth century could be defined through this concept of unlimited possibility, where 'we live in an almost infantile world where any demand, any possibility, whether for life-styles, travel, sexual roles and identities, can be satisfied instantly.'[146] As we've seen, in the twenty-first century the Cloud continues to be the subject of an intensified insistence that 'the only limits are your imagination', that anything goes. However, in contrast to Ballard's assertion that the 'terrifying casualty' of the century was a *death* of affect, the Cloud – as the high-point of and acceleration beyond what was once termed postmodernism – is actually the systematic management of an *excess* of affect. With the socio-technical nature of the contemporary milieu comes a deterritorialization of affect, something the evolution of an emergent Cloud ecology attempts to govern.

In the postmodern, 'habitual constellations of affect and patterns of movement' are partitioned into 'packets' which proliferate in the social field, only to actualize in new, unfamiliar combinations.[147] We might think of packet-switching as analogous to the means by which informatic-affect spreads through the host-parasite body, a viral resonance that occurs between divided-up affect packets distributed diffusely throughout the multitude. Information 'flow' occurs in a highly regulated fashion, ultimately a process aimed at *efficiency*, that is, by finding the most efficient route. The Cloud organizationally processes the complex problem of maintaining an overall flow of affective-labor by means of fragmentation and distribution, recombining input from a multiplicity of network nodes; as a system, its power draws on difference. In this sense, the process of reassembling, of packets combining together in new forms, is the translation of affect into the ability-to-act, into a collective emotional reaction, one that we might consider 'crowdsourced' and further determined by 'live' fluctuations to the overall noise of information flow. The individual body is less an originator and rather the receiver and transmitter of affect-packet messages. What then of the 'message' which these packets of information-affect transfer? It seems we can say that the relational ecology is the message, that *the Cloud is the message*. 'Affect has not become "flat"', Massumi insists, human existence 'has not been made unidimensional', but in contrast, the Cloud carefully manages an excess of affect to ensure continuing efficiency, particularly in regard to transmission, and this regulation requires a certain equivalence throughout the system, a beat by which affective heterogeneity can be controlled homogeneously. The machine remains soft, it has a pulse.

Part of this systemic efficiency means that the optimism of the twentieth century has today been displaced by an uneasiness and fear, where all the mind's possibilities continue to be explored but for the purposes of collective *self-management* rather than adventure – *we're all in this together*, after all. Here, 'radicalism' (affect unbound) is not completely opposed, instead it is something integral to the system, never fully out of control and thus fundamentally conservative. The question 'where do you want to go today?' becomes a means for ensuring affect is not waning or dying (i.e. becoming entropic) and, rather, that it responds to an affect-drop, continual injection towards meta-stability: a system driven by discontinuous productive intensification but one in which the sporadic becomes supervised. Affect is distributed and *amplified* rather than muted. The 'half-second' delay between action and cognition doesn't go undetected because it's insignificant or empty, but rather because it's 'overfull, in excess of the actually performed action and of its ascribed meaning.' Consciousness, and even volition or *will*, are 'subtractive' functions that 'reduce a complexity too rich to be functionally expressed.'[148] Yet the control implemented by the Cloud ensures that the level of this amplification has an integral peak and that any attempt to force an intensity beyond these levels becomes self-distorting. Here, then, the systemic efficiency of affect is defined by its complexity but one that seeks to draw order from chaos, it thus remains patterned and habitual, an addiction with a preconscious high. This amplification becomes an informatic white noise, a saturation of affect that appears to reach some kind of stable state, a levelling off. Principally this occurs in a fluctuation between positive and negative feedback, defined by cyberneticist Norbert Wiener as 'the property of being able to adjust future conduct by past performance'.[149] It's the flesh of the multitude, the 'interface' such as it is, that becomes fundamental to this feedback. As a result the body, besieged by affective forces, may actually become numbed: always-on, open to affective contagion from an archival ecology cum garden of forking paths, active 'choice' becomes anaesthetized, actions themselves seemingly inconsequential.

This sense is heightened when we consider the extent to which noise is also *temporal*. The informational 'atmosphere', the polyrhythm of the Cloud ecology is composed of the actual and virtual as they become simultaneous with each other. Data is not inert: it extends beyond itself, fecund with derivatives, disposed to 'mashing up' and always extrapolating. Multiple futures, multiple courses of action yet to be taken are mapped in the present. The Cloud as archive is not merely a database of the past or collection of memories, our habit-addiction and various 'affective autonomatisms' hyperlink to experience in advance.[150] We can consider the Cloud ecology as an affective territory, existence and behavior within the everyday subject to an underlying and continual modulation in the form of 'suggestions, mood enhancements, memory triggers, and reassurances.'[151] Indeed, this is Goodman's ecology of fear which seeks to manage the potential instabilities of the future(s). The multiplicity of threats with the potential to turn inward are thus handled in a qualitatively different manner. To merely await the arrival of the future means that actions will always be 'too late', only responding to events after they have already occurred, after the opportunity for total control has slipped by. Microsoft's Ballmer understands this, he wants us to commit our future, our 'digital life', to the Cloud, to come together and eradicate the trepidation of what's next. The multitude is made to *feel a responsibility* for the future. Like the affective fluctuations registered by stock markets, the Cloud as ecology extends an anthropomorphism into the everyday itself – our interface-less actions and reactions are predicated on a faith which in itself is preemptive and self-fulfilling. The body *infolds* the temporal.

In the Cloud, life exposed to an amplified modulation of affect takes on an auxiliary sense, intensively limited at the prepersonal level. Lanier hopefully proposes the power of resistance in what he describes as 'avatar-directed cognition'. This notion can, again, be seen in proto-form in a system like Microsoft's Kinect whereby the movement of the human body is measured by the console without the user having to wear any special devices or use other controller devices. Avatar-directed cognition would, moreover, enable the user to map their body onto other shapes, objects or things so as to aid learning. And yet, it seems increasingly the case that the individual body in the Cloud ecology is *already an avatar of itself*, or more specifically a temporal avatar. Indeed, 'avatar' is etymologically derived from the Sanskrit *avatāra*, meaning 'descent', and particularly the descent of the deity to an earthly manifestation. Our transition to this avatar-state is thus in alignment with the descent of the transcendental into the immanent, the 'descent' of the virtual into the actual and, increasingly, the descent of the future into the present.

Informatic noise, then, is comprised of permanent reverberations of the past (the affective ricochet of a vibrating archive in which present action must take place) but, equally, is made up of *resonances of the future*. So, not only are we ghostwritten by our data-doubles but, in this weird ecology, we also tune in to future-echoes, affective cadences which appear in the form of an informational foreshadow, increasingly blending with the atmosphere of the present. These ghostly resonances from polyrhythmic futures ultimately determine our state of readiness – our ability to act – regardless of whether specific futures ever become anything more than a temporal vibration of affect, regardless of whether they arrive in actuality. The 'event' itself becomes irrelevant. Our existence in the present increasingly takes on the performance of a virtual *already actualized* and merely held in abeyance as future shadow, a multiplicity of footsteps already laid out by our temporal avatar. Always-on is always-already. The increasingly more sophisticated incursions into the preconscious frontier 'cut' into the present in order to institute a preparedness, an inclination towards the future and, as Burroughs put it, 'when you cut into the present, the future leaks out.'[152] The microbiopolitical Cloud engages in a kind of temporal bloodletting, seeking to cure future disease or illness but, rather than seeking to eradicate these diseases, it undertakes a present inoculation. The ecology continually requires its own infection by the future, a boosting of its immunity. Drawing on these polyrhythmic futures, the body becomes adipose, seeking to contain the energy of potential while simultaneously feeding on it – this is a parasitical temporality which pre-digests or, better, *bleeds* the future.

# Chapter 3

# Reverse Obsolescence

*The future is but the obsolete in reverse.*
Vladimir Nabokov

*We are living in an era of low predictability ... Anything can happen.*
Tony Blair

## All Present and Correct, or, Shit to Gold

The scene presumably went something like this: Fade in. Microsoft Research Labs, early 2000s. Principal researcher Gordon Bell and his colleagues are celebrating the inception of their 'Total Recall' project. Sipping at sparkling wine from paper cups, they stand in a small crowd around Gordon's desk, a desk as significantly empty as his notice board and filing cabinets. Jim Gemmell, Gordon's trusted sidekick, raises the toast: 'Record everything, keep everything!' As the paper cups are clumped together with a cheer, Gordon captures the moment in his e-memory. This is it, he thinks to himself as the device monitoring his pulse detects a minor quickening. From here on in, every-thing will be born digital. For the past couple of years he and his assistants have been engaged in the laborious process of digitizing *every thing* in Gordon's life. A complete digital record of his life to this point – every piece of paper scanned, all audio and video ripped, every keepsake and souvenir photographed. But now, a clean slate, year zero. From tonight onwards he embarks upon CARPE: the Continuous Archival and Retrieval of Personal Experiences. Quite beyond the disordered and occasional activity of life blogging, this is full-spectrum, integrated and passive *life logging* – the automated capture and archiving of everything, with nothing discarded.[153] Hanging from a cord around his neck, Gordon wears a SenseCam, a tiny camera automatically producing photographs on a continuous timed cycle (say, every thirty seconds), or triggered by changes in ambient conditions (light, heat). Continuous, wirelessly archived audio and video will be the inevitable next step, he thinks, his body temperature raising slightly. Indeed, as Gordon Bell and Jim Gemmell state in their book, this project of 'Total Recall', this war against forgetfulness, lost memories and mislaid data aims to record and archive '... where you went, how you got there, who you met, what you did, what was said, how your vital signs varied, who you called, what you read, what you wrote, what you looked at ...'[154] And the size of data generated by all of this is irrelevant; according to 'Moore's Law', archival capacity for future memory continues to expand exponentially – the capacity of the Cloud has no limit. It is a project, of course, fundamentally aligned to the integrated efficiency brought about by cloud computing, the transformative power of which, according to Bell and Gemmell 'will be awesome.'

The emergent world these researchers are keen to herald is Stiegler's *mnemotechnological* world, where memory becomes subject to large-scale, industrial organization. Here, a memory-system functions as determinant of knowledge and truth; for the control society, it is the base of operations. Furthermore, we are drawn into another situation of paradoxical simultaneity, where forgetting gradually becomes impossible and yet we seem to remember less and less – cloud culture is both 'hypermnesia' and post-mnemonic.[155] The triumph of instantaneous inscription: *we both remember and forget everything*, embracing a forgetfulness underwritten by a fully-comprehensive mnemonic insurance. Indeed, *pace* Stiegler, memory-as-data operates in a möbius-like fashion – it's the Cloud ecology that is mnemonic. In such a world, we are increasingly deemed to be wholly reliant on an ability to interrogatively access this ecology – 'when your mind is absent, your e-memory is always there,' Bell and Gemmell insist – without the means to retrieve or read data, we are reduced to a bewildered abandonment, rendered simpletons.[156] As Nietzsche suggests in his writing on history, while it may be possible to live without access to memory and achieve a state of happiness, the form it takes will always be one of mindless contentment, herd-like mastication in the pastures of the present.[157]

Questions concerning technical amnesias are, however, only part of the much more crucial issue of temporality in play here, something that Bell and Gemmell's 'Grandpa's Secret Recipe' approach to technology utterly fails to mention. Quite the contrary in fact: amid the thicket of product endorsement, and following the obligatory seal of approval from Bill Gates, the 'e-memory revolution' emerges as the topic of gee-whizz gusto, carefully framed as nothing more than unpretentious, down-to-earth good sense. From the outset, the two researchers are keen to stress that this is an issue of *choice*: CARPE is something we will only embark upon willingly. And yet, we're equally told that this revolution is *inevitable*, that we are on 'an inexorable path to Total Recall technology' and that, in all likelihood, the devices we use now and those we will use in the future will engage us in this integrated act of passive archiving whether we like it or not, modulating the way we act in the world as a result.

The issue of choice, then, largely comes down to the constructed formation of that original 'clean slate'. Bell's 'complete record' of his life prior to instituting a practice of archival instantaneity remains the result of a reengineering process, selectively sculpting the ideal jumping-off point for a new self in a new model society. Inconveniences, irritations and embarrassments can be made to disappear. At year zero, every-thing lost to the archive at its moment of ontological inception is denied existence, lost to the barbarism of cultural construction of which Walter Benjamin warned.[158] From this moment though (the moment at which everything new is born digital), every action, response and thought is inscribed with permanence, an anti-forgetting, which, to call on the flipside of Nietzsche's contentedly grazing herd, institutes a situation in which it is 'altogether impossible to *live* at all.'[159] Without the power of forgetting, for all the data available to us, our contentment is rendered equally mindless – as for Borges's 'Funes the Memorious', the man from Fray Bentos whose existence is blighted – all hope of thought, even of sleep, shattered by the sheer vertigo of remembered detail, where life becomes something we can't understand, can't compute. The Cloud disturbs what we previously conceived as the delicate balance of history and memory, inverts it, even. Critically then, the instantaneous archive actually seeks to maintain year zero as an eternal state of being, futures are pulled into the present in an effort to adhere to this hygiene of time. For all the rhetoric concerning brave new worlds, the Cloud archive induces a slowing down, a cataclysmic crystallization, a stubborn refusal to move forward and rather an insistence that the future(s) are instead moved toward us. One thinks of the drained vapidity, the burnt-out, desertified banality of Ballard's imagined futures – the Crystal World coated and engorged with time, pasts and futures ornamentally fused together, or equally, Robert Smithson's 'New Monumentality', in which the excremental Babel of the contemporary archive constitutes a vast entropy machine, and 'lethargy is elevated to the most glorious magnitude.'[160]

As a consequence, the weaving together of a multiplicity of digital traces to construct an ever denser information shadow represents something of a small step; what appears revolutionary is the forecast torrent of increased data generated by innumerable sources, the thickening and expansion of the shadow, and the means by which it will feed back into future production. This is, after all, *recall* and not just retention, archiving as a two-way cybernetic process, explicitly shaping our being in the world. The institution then, of an algorithmic temporality, in which virtuals (data-extrapolation of archived past actions) generate actuals (action in the present) cybernetically. As 'librarian, archivist, cartographer, and curator' of our own lives, we enter into an ontological pragmatism, a life-management routine, where everything about ourselves can be 'chronicled, condensed, cross-correlated and plotted out' in order to yield '[h]igher productivity and more vitality, longer life spans, deeper and wider knowledge of our world.'[161] This is Jacques Derrida's *archiving archive*, a protocological and algorithmically driven process of inscription, modulated for productive efficiency which serves to determine the nature of 'archivable' content 'even as it is coming into existence', indeed, this archiving process 'produces as much as it records the event.'[162] Our 'invention' occurs within the video-game mode of production, necessarily pre-figured by the Cloud; as before, we create and perceive our world simultaneously. The days when our self-chronicling was 'haphazard', 'non-systematic', will soon be behind us. CARPE then, or Total Recall, is the quest for a life *pattern*, the Cloud as archive offers a means of interrogating, mining and sifting through the offensive chaos of our lives in order to impose an order and efficiency upon it ... 'What would happen if you could take that whole slurry of life-history fragments and run it all through a powerful pattern-detection program? What kinds of patterns might you find?'[163] Or, more pertinently, how might those patterns be put to use? At this banalized cybernetic frontier of the post-human, our 'life slurry' stands ready for filtering into smooth and efficient flow. No more inefficient lumps, no more messy bits. Concerned? Fear not – the philosophical and ethical model to follow here, is that of capitalist indifference: 'In the world of business, we do not hear arguments against record keeping or concerns that facing the truth is inferior to a comfortably dimmed memory. Accountants do not spend their lunch breaks debating the need to forget or whether storing every single transaction might clutter the record too much.'[164] And, if the assurances of these pragmatic accountants don't convince you, know that facing this hyper-statistical systemic and relativistic 'truth' is, of course, 'the price of self-improvement.'[165]

Memory-connectivity is both extensive and intensive; the various devices Bell and Gemmell propose are merely the technical prototypes for an entryway, a means of accessing the archive, provisionally a pocket device until it disappears entirely, fuses with the body itself. E-memories 'follow us on our travels,' even (and especially in the context of a collective Cloud memory) those memories which are not our own. Indeed, capital encourages a continually shifting identity turnover ... *become other* ... be whoever or whatever we want to be.[166] Thus, what had been territorial *aides-mémoire* are now set in a state of constant exchange and realignment, subject to a dynamically integrated interaction amid the upheaval of the mnemonic commons. Private coordinates exist only in assemblage; the Cloud instils its own background locus of homogeneous familiarity. But Bell and Gemmell's insistence that this 'intimate extension' of biological memory adjusts and advances it into something new – something which conditions our present – fails to consider the degree to which this is merely a conditioning towards nihilism.[167] The permanence of inscription is equally a mark of futility. An archival ontology is one in which experience is differentiated from that already recorded and tagged on the level of minutiae: faced with endlessly forking paths, infinite potential, our actions in fact become typological, differences only made apparent within the context of the recorded data set. Unlike Alice (and latterly, *The Matrix's* Neo), we take *both* the red and blue pill simultaneously, and they react together as placebo effect.

Key in this respect is what Bell and Gemmell prophesize as software of 'automatic summarization' – systems in which both the micro and macro elements of life would be systemically examined for *novelty*, highlighting and utilizing the unusual – the *new* – and consigning everything else – the average, the mundane

– to the recesses of the archive. Auto-summarization is pitched as a process of indispensable biographization that will 'reduce the chores involved in making one's life bits *worthwhile to others*,' others like the system itself, and particularly the curiously anthropomorphized figure of *posterity* who 'will be able to browse your e-memories starting from a manageable "birds-eye" view of a life, rather than just confronting an intimidating jungle of material.'[168] We have said already that the power of the Cloud is that of definition, the governance of truth, knowledge and thus the ability to act. As archive, this is most evident in its concern with the *everyday*. Indeed, we could fundamentally align the methodology of the Cloud with that of the experimental writer Georges Perec. In *An Attempt at Exhausting a Place in Paris*, Perec presents an archive of Place Saint-Sulpice in Paris over one weekend in 1974, described in exhaustive detail. His intention here is to reject that which is typically deemed 'significant' and rather to focus on the remainder, that which goes by unnoticed. This process of questioning the habitual, especially when one is habituated to it, is in itself, an unnatural, disorienting perhaps even painful experience. In Peter Handke's novel *The Goalie's Anxiety at the Penalty Kick*, it can be like 'seeing someone walk toward the door and instead of looking at the man you looked at the doorknob. It made your head hurt, and you couldn't breathe properly any more.'[169] Unlike the distributed assemblage, it would require a resilience from the ordinary observer to maintain this kind of outlook for long. Perec's aim in capturing the totality of a defined Parisian space is to thus expose 'that which we generally don't notice, which doesn't call attention to itself, which is of no importance.'[170] In this exposure, the scene is revealed as one that modulates constantly, refusing to be reduced to mere background, becoming instead something more noteworthy. Here, the novelty, the new, constantly changes but it can equally arise from the existing slurry of the habitual, newly *revealed*. The Cloud hears Perec's call. We live the habitual 'as if it weren't the bearer of any information' he says; the Cloud, on the contrary, precisely targets these 'common things', filtering them from a life slurry or 'wrest[ing] them from the dross in which they remain mired', as Perec has it. Defining and redefining the dross, until it's no longer dross. Summarization, a kind of archival alchemy, is equally a means to reveal and utilize the formerly hidden surplus value. Consequently, the Cloud enacts a systemic rendering of Perec's anthropology of the self, the multitude undertake an archival ontology, seeking to record and describe 'the banal, the quotidian ... the background noise, the habitual' or as Perec fittingly puts it, the *infra-ordinary*.[171]

Clearly though, Perec fails in his attempt – while his archive is a document of unstructured description, capturing the constant modulation of the space during the weekend in which the observation took place, the Parisian location itself can never be fully *exhausted* and instead continues to generate new material for the archivist. The micro level can always be magnified at still greater power, further bifurcations always remain; in control societies, there is no closure, no completion. Yet the Cloud archive relies precisely upon this fact, the truly average or mundane would prove unproductive and thus entropic, a failure. To avoid this calcification it must grow ever more immediate in its capture and draw ever closer in its analysis, subdividing the ordinary into the infra-ordinary, revealing the magnificence of the vernacular, poring over the background noise. The trivial and the futile must be mined for surplus value, the multitude remain informational raw material. The birds-eye view of life is only possible once that life has first been dissected. Yet, as Perec's intense scrutinizing becomes ever more detailed he also becomes lost, perhaps intentionally, in his own archive: 'By looking at only a single detail ... and for a sufficiently long period of time (one or two minutes), one can, without any difficulty, imagine that one is in Etampes or in Bourges or even, moreover, in some part of Vienna where I've never been.'[172] The way in which we contend with such a lost state is crucial. We can no more yearn for a prophylactic cleansing, embracing a destructive nihilism as means to escape the information traumas of the Cloud: 'one almost begins to wish for the ancient destructive amnesias of the fire at the celebrated library of Alexandria.'[173] But, equally, the surrender to a *dérive*, a nihilistic passivity of numbing aimlessness offers only a dead end.

Of course, such software, as part of the underlying logic of the Cloud ecology, could not merely seek to ensure an organized and detailed personal archive *post-mortem*. Instead, in its continuous definition of the infra-ordinary, it would also effect a phatic reductionism on action, constantly and newly defining states of averageness, thus demanding an ever more meticulous dissection in order to recategorize a modulating 'new'. Furthermore, and crucially, Bell and Gemmell conceive of this software as a means for visualizing life as a 'time line' which emphasizes the 'best material' or 'memory landmarks'. In a process of continual feedback these memory landmarks would become pre-empted, events on the extended time line flagged up as future material of novelty, moments at which life undertakes the production of the new so important to the archive. The Microsoft researchers complain of the social prejudice against 'keeping everything' – in doing so one is viewed as a hoarder, they insist, 'obsessed with your past'.[174] We might summon to mind those OCD sufferers depicted in TV's *Life of Grime*, recluses filling refrigerators with bottles of piss, sedimenting their living spaces with a compost of used toilet paper and newspapers laid down over decades. Of course, Bell and Gemmell are only half right (or half wrong). Hoarding, particularly the (never ending) quest for an exhaustive, totalizing archive, actually represents *an orientation toward and obsession with the future*, one that impacts critically on the present, defining and shaping actions around future mnemonic events.

## Saved!

Bell and Gemmell are anything but shy in placing the issue of *digital immortality* at the forefront of their sales pitch for an instantaneous archival ontology; it's not difficult to detect the techno-messianic rhetoric which saturates much of the commentary on this emergent cloud culture and further defines our faith-based post-political landscape. With the digitization of 'legacy media' and the installation of new sources of instantaneous, passive e-memory, we're told that the next step for our digital memories will be investment in an avatar, thus enabling the narcissistic 'bequeathing' of our 'ideas, deeds, and personality to posterity...'[175] Further, this avatar will be one that 'future generations can speak with and get to know' as the life-pattern revealed by archival analysis – the rationalized order from chaos – describes the program of our decision-making, opinion formation and affective preconscious responses, all of which will enable the configuration of a 'two-way immortality' whereby the avatar responds as we would have in biological life and can even *learn* and *develop* in the same way.[176] Living on in post-biological form, throwing off the clumsy materiality of our corporeal bodies, this is the gospel of the *Singularity*.

The Singularity is the moment, fabled by futurists, at which human and machine coalesce and henceforth act as one in actuality, the distributed intelligence of a system with a state of awareness resulting in humankind's transcendence from the biological. Ray Kurzweil, grand magus of this movement, believes the Cloud marks the beginning of this process of transcendence, enabling us to break from the confines of the brain's limited neurons (a mere hundred billion) and instead transform thinking into networked computation – Cloud ecology as super-brain.[177] Nonetheless, as demonstrated by the induction of the increasingly post-human multitude into the systemic assemblage of cloud computing, a certain kind of singularity has already taken place.

Shaviro's critique of Kurzweil is salient. Kurzweil, on the face of it, is 'overtly anti-religious' and, equally, his utopianism is apolitical and asocial.[178] He presents a bright but utterly shallow future, never bothering himself with questions of the socio-political, other than to suggest that the Singularity will enable humankind to 'rise above' the complications of a globalized world. Technology conquers all. A utopianism stripped of radicalism proves itself incapable of escaping a general extrapolation of an already existing state of affairs and Kurzweil's SF realist vision for the fourth dimension remains itself one-dimensional. And yet, the Singularity remains a concept defined by a fervent, devotional zeal, equivalent to the Christian Rapture – the transference of the soul to heaven prior to the approaching apocalypse, the *end of time*. As Jaron Lanier makes clear, the Singularity necessitates 'people dying in the flesh and being uploaded into a computer and remaining conscious, or people simply being annihilated in an imperceptible instant before a new super-consciousness takes over the Earth. The Rapture and the Singularity share one thing in common: they can never be verified by the living.'[179] *Beware* then, the futurists, who would make us slave to our avatar, sacrifice us to immortality, incarcerate us within a present satiated with past and future.

## When the Schizophrenic Connects the Dots

There is value in the virtual. We have already stated that the Cloud draws upon a dynamic invention-power, upon the *potential* of the networked multitude, social labor as a source of innovation and creation. Value is ultimately defined through the 'pull of the future', focused on the state of the present in the context of *how things will be*.[180] And yet, potential also represents an inherent threat to the system, a latent force of destabilization. As a control assemblage of capital and security, the Cloud is the manifestation of a contemporary power that is increasingly *pre-emptive* – in the bleak aftermath of the Bush-Blair era, society continues to be defined by concerns of security, of guaranteeing future states, seizing the new, negating the unknown. Shocks or disruptions to the system of creative production must be counteracted *before* they arise, informational exchange and the future flow of data must be assured through continual micro-management. Consequently the state of 'normality' must remain under constant review, 'the imaginative geography of the deviant, atypical, abnormal other' must be reinscribed '*inside* the spaces of daily life', inside the archive.[181] Mutant delinquencies are planned for, absorbed into a systemic framework which itself undergoes transformation as part of this process of reinscription. Indeed, rather than submitting to the magnetism of the future, the Cloud is the means by which the immediate future can be secured and colonized here in the present, by pulling the future into the everyday, actualizing its value.

Security is driven by a need to identify and manage what US Secretary of Defense Donald Rumsfeld notoriously defined as *unknown unknowns*. The real danger, he suggested, is found less in those things 'we know ... we do not know' and rather in 'the ones we don't know we don't know.'[182] The target here is that which escapes a process of 'recording everything, keeping everything' and even 'analyzing everything'. Indeed, analysis has become ineffectual, the issue here is one concerning the most efficient and extensive capture and control of invention-power, the harnessing of *imagination*. Accordingly, as Department of Defense memos reveal, in the days immediately following the 9/11 attacks Deputy Secretary Paul Wolfowitz, decried a 'failure of the imagination' in the intelligence services.[183] The 9/11 Commission Report too, suggests that, given previous intelligence relating to a potential terrorist plot involving an 'explosives-laden' aircraft, this failure of the imagination, this inability to conceive aircraft-as-weapon, requires urgent reversal via *the institutionalization of the imagination process*. It's crucial, the report states 'to find a way of routinizing, even bureaucratizing, the exercise of imagination.'[184] Imagination becomes key to securing all kinds of unknowns. As a result, Wolfowitz's earlier memo to Rumsfeld entitled 'Preventing More Events' – in which he stoked the fires for a forthcoming invasion of Iraq – should better have read *pre-empting all events.*[185] The institutionalized imagination is the power to diagram the future, to think and act transversally; as the 9/11 Commission reports states, '[t]he importance of integrated, all-source analysis cannot be overstated. Without it, it is not possible to "connect the dots." No one component holds all the relevant information.'[186]

The Cloud, of course, represents the coming of this institutionalized, integrated imagination, its very purpose being to make pre-emptive connections in order to contain radical events *within* the system and thus deny their radicalism, to 'translate *probable* associations…into *actionable* security decisions' or what we might otherwise understand as the endeavour to enclose and delimit futurity in the bureaucratized present.[187] And yet, despite the bluster of the so-called '1% doctrine' where even the slightest suspicion of risk or danger is quashed in a pre-emptive strike, cloud culture simultaneously relies upon harnessing an underlying and continual state of risk inherent to an economy of anxiety and unease; the Cloud, like the markets it consumes, operates with an internally contained radicalism. The Cloud-as-archive is the means by which, through multiplicitous connection, this risk is managed and controlled, by which threats are 'imagineered' and diagrammed, absorbed rather than eliminated.

Pre-emptive power has, of course, a multifarious genealogy which can be traced variously in Cold War military strategy 'games', computer scenario modelling, insurance risk assessment and neoliberal financial speculation. Indeed, the strategy of pre-emption shares some methods with the latter of these relations – speculation – in as much as it is a technique of the Cloud system intended to simultaneously foresee and encourage targeted volatility as a means of control.[188] Further, a database or archival ecology is defined by the exploitation of debt as a productive medium, the Cloud is a temporal landlord and we are in debt to the future. Nonetheless, pre-emptive power does not take the form of hedging against unexpected risk, rather it seeks to generate the actual from the virtual, to bring about and control risks in order to negate the possibility of mutative shocks being unforeseen. Seize the value by causing risk to occur under terms pre-defined by a system in place to deal with it. In this, the inception of the future is a form of algorithmic security which dispenses with mere prediction. Indeed, the continual production of the new is balanced alongside a securing and safeguarding of the pre-empted present by identifying potential-ities immanent to that present and acting upon them, *regardless of whether they in fact come about*. Indeed, pre-emptive power precisely concerns the induction of future consequences in the present quite apart from eventual actuality. These are 'affective facts' – the *consequences* of the future made present.[189] The relationship between contemporary technology and memory (and thus, time) exceeds the merely cybernetic, exceeds deter-ministic linearity. A significant departure from forecasting then, this is a process of *imagining* what Richard Grusin describes as 'multiple futures which are alive in the present, which always exist as not quite fully formed potentialities or possibilities.'[190] Imagining future *value*, then, which can be induced, actualized – acted upon and secured – in the present. In this respect, the systematic modulation between degrees of passive and radical imagining is a proliferation of control throughout the ontological into the virtual.

Yet the Cloud employs a mode of pre-emption to exploit invention-power in a manner that's more fantastic than a mere extrapolation of the empirical; instead it seeks to promote, to quote SF author John Wyndham, a 'wild riot of pointless imaginings,' which, here, occurs as a rationalized appropriation of the pathological, converting the performative actions and behavior of psycho-social instability, Ballard's 'energizing potential,' into a productive activity.[191] Indeed, cloud time in its crystal form has a significance equivalent to that fundamental synchronization and regularization of labor which took place during the industrial revolution. The temporal schizophrenia inherent to life in this new archival ecology (the simultaneous existence in the present of a multiplicity of possible futures) has a productive capacity; as the virtual is increasingly collapsed into the actual mental states become as 'real', if not more so, as external empirical 'reality'. In order to defend against failures of the imagination, the invention-power of the multitude is put to work in a regime of continual training, through which imaginings can become wilder, more riotous.

According to Elsaesser, this productive pathology is a symptom evident in forms of twenty-first century entertainment, notably, as we've already mentioned, the 'mind-game film', the symptoms of which we can equally detect in a number of recent 'high-concept' SF drama series, all of which are centred on themes of temporality.[192] For Elsaesser, the mind-game film features a protagonist not only distinctly unreliable as a narrator, but mentally or psychologically unstable, often exhibiting symptoms of paranoia, schizophrenia and/or amnesia. We can detect similarities in *Heroes, Flashforwards* and particularly *Lost,* the latter of which features a gradually increasing cast of characters in a sprawling narrative revolving around the survivors of a passenger aircraft crashed on a strange Pacific island. From the outset the programme begins with episodic narratives occurring on parallel timelines – the island in the present and the various pasts of characters' lives prior to the plane crash. In later series, rather than becoming familiar, these individual characters break up into component alterities, they become unstable within the narrative (experiencing, together with the general mysteriousness of the island, the bewilderment and paranoia of numerous McGuffins and temporal shifts) and unstable as representations (fragmented schizo-characters that we as an audience cannot rely upon).[193] Our efforts to find a *solution* to this puzzle, de- and re-constructing the narrative by piecing together information in new relational sequences, becomes comparable to interacting with a database or an archive, something that requires new, non-linear types of thought, new processes of imagining, whole new methods of connecting the dots. Crucially then, rather than seeking to bolster the 'contract' between the programme and audience which suggests there will be no 'lying' to the viewer, these mind-game programmes seek to enact within the audience the very condition from which the protagonists suffer.[194]

With new systems of organizing attention invoking carefully modulated paranoid or schizophrenic relations, these are programmes that require dedication and concentration from the audience (the pilot episode of *The Event*, for example, moves rapidly between several timelines) but also engagement that expands considerably beyond the time spent watching the programme. The productive relationship in which the audience is engaged leads to exploration not only concerning the narrative but, Elsaesser argues, questions concerning epistemology or ontology. *Lost* operates as a mythos, a network of concepts (the mysterious Hanso corporation, various numeric sequences) which enter into dynamic propagation and evolution across various media platforms, including a number of Alternate Reality Games which, during its production, served to feed back into the programme itself. Work is required in order to enter this world, to discover its secret levels; understanding it fully comes about only through creative analysis engendered as a social process. As a case in point, *Lost* rewards devotion with ever greater narrative complexity: later episodes feature a continual and separate narrative branched off in the future, a temporal bifurcation whereby we see the same characters in two different time periods and even an alternative version of the present. Narratives therefore become increasingly puzzling rather than moving toward an obvious conclusion, attention turns to supposition and game playing with the distribution of clues and red herrings. Elsaesser points to the fact that the audiences' active engagement with the puzzle of meaning entails 'constant retroactive revision, new reality checks, displacements, and reorganization not only of temporal sequence, but of mental space ...'[195] An archival or database ontology brings about the disintegration of chronological causality, past and future are folded into the present, temporality also taking on the now familiar form of the möbius. Here then, we 'discover' or newly invent connections in a process of thought that not only disregards empirical reality but also linearity and causality; imagining and inventing occurs in experimental and lateral fashion, employing intuition, continually developing a conceptual toolbox of increasing complexity, alterity, multidimensional extension.

Extending this slightly, we might also say that engagement is driven by distributed affect, impelled by a state of normalized anxiety – as long as we are unable to fully understand the totality of connections, the multiplicity of ways in which dots of data can be combined together, the future remains unknown and thus dangerous. A symptom of the Cloud ecology is 'the generalized condition of time anomaly, generated by the swirling weather system of looped media,' an anomalous temporality in which linear thinking is increasingly rendered inept if not chaotic.[196] The consequential need to attain understanding through increasingly pathologized imagining is due to the modulation of this general fear, evident not least in the domestication of 'terror' – alert statuses can suddenly rise, our anticipatory levels of vigilance must become more active.[197] The affective fact: the fear of instability becomes destabilizing. Our pre-emptive imagining is a vigilance-machine, a state of network readiness that secures future crises in the present. Pure rationality is no longer effective; the Cloud requires a multitude functioning through a rationalized-psychopathology.

As 'production techniques' these are, of course, the very strategies of resistance proposed by Deleuze and Guattari as means to negate the socializing power of capitalism. The schizophrenic, in an experimental plunge into 'the realm of deterritorialization ... deliberately seeks out the very limit of capitalism.'[198] Rather than some kind of incapacity or weakness that limits the schizophrenic's ability to exist in the world, he or she possesses an ability to engage with that world in ways previously *unimagined*. By instituting a temporal security apparatus in the form of this future-present, breakdowns become breakthroughs, secure expansions of the system. In a promotion of database thinking, the Cloud institutes that only hinted at by the mind-game programme – the operation of a testing and training ground for the development of productive, cognitive skills, all of which are definitively aligned to the neo-liberal requirement to remain adaptive, flexible, proactive and responsive to change. Moreover, cloud *games* are those with rules, those which result in the pre-emptive imagining of present future(s) while producing subjects of capital which can be thought of as having a cognitive efficiency suited to this new temporality. Nonetheless, this new efficiency remains highly controlled, once the limits of capital have been explored there is always a consequent reterritorialization. In this, the institutionalization of imagination is a process which feeds back on itself, instilling a temporal localization.

Therefore, while there may appear to be any number of narrative trajectories through an open archive or database, the socialization of pathologies in new productive modes remain 'anthropomorphized versions of mathematical code and automated programs.'[199] Similarly, Bell and Gemmell's project of life as instantaneous archival process requires the adoption of a controlled productive pathology – action occurs alongside a simultaneous computation of how it might relate and connect to everything already part of the archive and everything yet to become inscribed within it. Trajectories of action with the data ecology of the Cloud are thus always deferred, associational, immediacy becomes anticipation. Productive imagining of alternative connections continually grows in complexity and sophistication but ultimately remains within an architecture of imagination-control, 'there is no point of immunity or safety from which one might safely create a "pure" image of the future,' our imaginations of the future always have a built-in obsolescence.[200] In imagining and absorbing the multiplicity of possible worlds the Cloud presents itself as a totality, a map of all possible futures, albeit one that is constantly expanding, updating. With the cooptation and adoption of everything imaginable – even or especially futures that are in conflict with each other, contradictory – anything unimaginable itself becomes lost. As before, we are 'banned' from the fullness of the virtual, subject to a state of exception. Grusin and others suggest that the future will have been pre-imagined and systemically acted upon by the time it finally 'emerges into the present' but the möbius-temporality brought about by the Cloud disallows any 'arrival' by inducing its coexistence.[201] When the virtual is always already actual there's no longer anything that remains to 'emerge'.

## Formatting the Future, or, The Ghost is (in) the Machine

An allegory of the Cloud: Tom McCarthy's novel *Remainder* – narrative existentialism ostensibly in the Sartrean or Kafkaesque vein, but equally a kind of alter-SF, a ricochet off Ballard and Dick set in contemporary Brixton. The story concerns the life of an unnamed narrator following an ambiguous accident. Something, we are told, fell from the sky. This snatch of detail is, in itself, open to question, but the narrator cannot tell us more – as part of his multi-million pound settlement deal he is legally bound never to discuss the particulars of the incident. Not that he is able to discuss it even if he wished; awakening from some months of coma he has to recover not only from bodily injuries but also from gaps and flaws in his memory. Indeed, he is forced to consciously *relearn that which was never learnt*, that which had always been natural, instilled through the process of life: movement, recollection and, crucially, existence in the present. The memories that do return come to him like a series of mundane filmic sequences, to which he feels passively disconnected, 'It could have been another history, another set of actions and events, like when there's been a mix-up and you get the wrong holiday photos back from the chemist's. I wouldn't have known or cared differently, and would have accepted them the same.'[202]

There are, then, two early turning points for the narrator. The first is a crisis over his own inauthenticity: the self-consciousness of his movements and actions, the extent to which he feels himself to be 'plastic' rather than malleable, incapable of entering into 'the flow', detecting a layer between himself and the actions he carries out. All of which renders his affective responses artificial, second hand, false. The second, and major, turning point occurs while at a house party. Escaping the banality and boredom of the evening he retreats to the bathroom where he comes across a crack in the wall, a fractured, urban madeleine, the discovery of which triggers an intense jolt of *déjà-vu*, a 'crystal clear' memory. The crack sparks a powerful sequence of memories concerning a building he has seemingly lived in at some point in the past, a recalled sequence complete with precise details of events that could be seen from his window, the sounds and smells wafting in from other apartments, encounters with residents in the corridor, even the specific way in which the sun falls on the floor. A visualization of the mundane of which Perec would be proud. More than anything, it's a memory-*hit*; he has a strong affective response to the sense of authentic existence, lived non-consciously. In this earlier lost time and space he had 'merged with his gestures', or as he puts it 'run through them and let them run through me until there'd been no space between us'.[203] It remains, however, nothing more than *déjà-vu*, a sense of having experienced this sequence of events in the past, but a sense laden with doubt as to whether it is a 'memory' at all, or something more complex: 'Maybe it was various things all rolled together: memories, imaginings, films ...'[204]

The evolution or transformation of time described in this chapter, a move away from clock time and linear causality toward something else, a *cloud time*, is then the literal demonstration of Henri Bergson's theses, as elucidated by Deleuze – our body clock, or internal sense of time should no longer be considered primary, rather it increasingly yields to a temporal ecology: '... it is we who are internal to time, not the other way round ... Time is not the interior in us, but just the opposite, the interiority in which we are, in which we move, live and change.'[205] The Bergsonian concept of time is one in which the actual and virtual coalesce in unity. Here, the present comprises both present and past together, as Deleuze puts it, '[t]he past does not follow the present that it is no longer, it coexists with the present it was.' Consequently, for Bergson, *déjà-vu* or 'paramnesia' is the demonstration of this coalescence – we 'remember' the present in the present, something Bergson aligns to a performance:

> Every moment of our life presents two aspects, it is actual and virtual, perception on the one side and recollection on the other ... Whoever becomes conscious of the continual duplicating of his present into perception and recollection ... will compare himself to an actor playing his part automatically, listening to himself and beholding himself playing.[206]

However, the Cloud complicates this conceptual schema. In cloud time the coalescence of the actual and virtual becomes concentrated, a Ballardian congealing or condensation, the present comprises not only the present and past but also the future – the future coexists with the present it is not yet.[207] This is a temporality of '[e]verything that's ever happened, all the events that will ever happen ... taking place together.'[208] Here then, paramnesia is equally a remembering of, or a nostalgia for, the future in the present. In this respect, the rationalization that Bell and Gemmell are keen to promote stands in opposition to what they consider *confabulation*, namely the creation of false memories or even the *confusion of the imagination with memory* (also the essential meaning of paramnesia). The syndrome of 'false memory' is cited as a strong justification to 'record everything, keep everything', a defense, a system of security against powers of the false.[209] Nonetheless, rather than an unintended *con*fusion, the Cloud invokes a *fusion* of imagination with memory as the multitude become the means by which an integrated system can inventively pre-empt memories of the future(s). The temporality of the Cloud institutes a rationalized fabulation, a complete relativism or general equivalence between actual and virtual. In Ballard's words, 'nothing is true and nothing is untrue.'[210]

In this condensed present of excess, we might say that the 'performance' to which Bergson alludes is *hauntological*, the Cloud ecology is populated by ghosts, but here the ghost appears as a spectre of the future. As Derrida suggests, the spectre is a symbol of paradox, neither present nor absent, living nor dead, soul nor body, yet also each of these.[211] Certainly an archival ontology necessitates living alongside and amongst ghosts of the past, and in their announcement that the coming world of 'Total Recall' will 'change our intimate relationships with loved ones both living and dead,' Bell and Gemmell seek to intensify the degree to which we turn to this spectral data for advice as much as it whispers in our ear.[212] Yet in the Cloud ecology, time is still further out of joint. The *habitual*, the pattern, is pulled from the future and conjured in the present for us to adopt – our algorithmic existence is therefore replete with *déjà-vu* as pre-emptive programming effects modulations to the habitual atmosphere of the present. Tasks 'that are never done for the first time ... will always need to be done again,' the everyday has become electronically 'spectralized'.[213] Haunted by both the past and multiple, contradictory futures, the condensed present is a temporality of control, defined by a state of hauntological formatting.

In *Remainder*, the narrator's memory sequence can be read as taking on such a formatting function. Having received a vast sum of compensation from his accident, he has the funds in order to actualize his 'memory', to re-enact it so as to experience again the affective resonance of 'reality'. He purchases an apartment building and has it remodelled to precisely match his visual-ization, after which he employs a group of amateur performers to take on the characters of the building's residents, each person carefully chosen to correspond to his memory sequence. Following a series of rehearsals the building can then be switched to 'on mode', actors, or as the narrator insists, *re-enactors*, actualize the hauntologically back-projected sequence as a continual loop: a man tinkers with a motorbike outside, never completing his repairs; a pianist continually plays the same piece of music, intentionally going wrong at the same point each time; an old woman cooks liver all day so as to infuse an olfactory ambience. McCarthy's narrator then moves through the spaces of the building at will, engaging with this interactive *tableau vivant* of the everyday, his body gliding 'fluently and effortlessly through the atmosphere around it' deciphering the patterns of its flow, moving in harmony with the enclosed temporal ecology.[214] This is action without action – like McCarthy's narrator, we receive an affective hit for en-acting and becoming in tune with the pre-empted pattern.

The narrator's forensic obsession with the patterns of flow in this space requires the totality of sequence-components to be inventoried and deciphered, a methodical atomisation, 'breaking down ... movements into phases that have sections and sub-sections, each one governed by rigorous rules.' He gathers, or 'captures', data – patches of oil, angles against walls, the period of time it takes for swings in the courtyard to come to a state of rest after being pushed with a certain force – maximising the use value of surplus, the stains of existence, but, unlike Perec, in the knowledge that it cannot be exhausted. We not only behold ourselves playing the part, as Bergson suggested, but we scrutinize our performance in constant pre-hearsals, layering and condensing our investment in the infra-ordinary, logging and archiving, remembering to forget, all in an effort to lose ourselves *inside* the role. Even within the fixed set of elements of his *tableau vivant*, his contrived 'event' as a repeating sequence, McCarthy's narrator continues to break down his interactions into their constituent parts – he runs the building in 'on mode' with the actors executing their pre-formatted roles but at a continually reduced speed – the better a pattern is understood, the easier it can be fulfilled, adhered to passively, non-consciously. Thus, in a display of increasingly pathological tendencies, he can become lost in these ever deeper layers of what Perec called the 'endotic', performing an anthropology of enclosed temporality. In cloud time, failure to fulfil the format renders us unreal, inauthentic, out of sequence with the patterned flows of affect which govern life. The filtering of our life slurry aims to transform it into something *recognisable*, the desire here is to stop being 'separate, removed, imperfect.'[215]

So, in cloud time there is a stretching, an elongation of the present along a horizon, monumentalized, crystalline, like ice. In the world of Bell and Gemmell's *instantaneous* archiving, the interval has shrunk to disappearance, there is no time to enact other than in the present, we must remain aware, in tune, attentive. Yet the moment which is so fleeting is also the moment condensed and encompassing, a microtemporality that becomes the macro. Addicted to the affective-joy of passivity, we seek a continual merger with the space around us, to lose ourselves in non-consciousness, *strung out*. In the dissected pattern of a widening and expanding ever-present, this passivity of action, thinking and relationality takes on a stasis, we willingly enter an affective fugue state, drifting, as with McCarthy's narrator, 'towards the edge of a trance'.[216] Enclosed in this utopia of the infra-ordinary, the multitude enters a fugue of passive nihilism, assemblage crystallising as apparatus. The propagation and mushrooming of the present, continually unfolding from the repetition and extension of the infra-ordinary imbues the everyday with 'an almost sacred aspect'.[217] Indeed, in the zealous transferral of life to the archive, including that life yet to occur, the Cloud seems to pull even the Singularity into the present, bureaucratizing the clutter of matter so as to move ever closer to a transubstantiation, a dematerialization, a moment of permanent uploading within and surrender to the pattern.[218]

Just as with the conclusion to *Remainder*, in cloud time our space of re/pre-enactment has no edges: there is no point at which we step out of this ecology, we find ourselves temporally enclosed, spectres of the future becoming increasingly corporeal. We were lost in the wilderness. We have been saved.

# Coda

*In a hermit's writings, you can always hear something of the echo of the desert, something of the whisper and the timid sideways glance of solitude. A new and more dangerous type of silence, of concealment, rings out in his strongest words, even in his cries. Anyone who has sat alone with his soul in intimate dispute and dialogue, year in, and year out, day and night, anyone who has become a cave bear or treasure hunter or treasure guard and dragon in his cave (which might be a labyrinth but also a gold mine): his very concepts will come to acquire their own twilight colour, the smell of depth just as much as of mildew, something uncommunicative and reluctant that blows a chill on everything going past. The hermit does not believe that a philosopher – given that a philosopher was always a hermit first – has ever expressed his actual and final opinions in books: don't people write books precisely to keep what they hide to themselves? In fact, he will doubt whether a philosopher could even have 'final and actual' opinions, whether for a philosopher every cave does not have, must not have, an even deeper cave behind it – a more extensive, stranger, richer world beyond the surface, an abyss behind every ground, under every 'groundwork'. Every philosophy is a foreground philosophy – that is a hermit's judgment: 'There is something arbitrary in his stopping here, looking back, looking around, in his not digging any deeper here, and putting his spade away – there is also something suspicious about it.' Every philosophy conceals a philosophy too: every opinion is also a hiding place, every word is also a mask.*

Friedrich Nietzsche

Our *dramatis personae* remain enclosed in the stretched and crystallized present, *tableaux vivants* of fugue ontology. Steve Ballmer is at the front of a packed, fluorescently lit lecture theatre, in the middle of the stage, mid-strut, the fingers of his hands splayed as if searching the air for something tangible to grab hold of, something with which to emphasize an empty point. Charles Leadbeater, waiting for his next flight, stands at the airport window overlooking the runways, his head held high, skies reflected in eyes focused on the mushroom cloud blooming on the horizon. Gordon Bell and Jim Gemmell are frozen in their laboratory, their raised paper cups pushing against one another with microscopic velocity as they long for the occurrence of events that might be recorded.

It has seemed to us to make most sense to fabulate the Cloud, rather than dwell upon any technical specification. McCarthy, Perec, Ballard, Lovecraft and suchlike have been our resources, as much as those theorists we have cited. They can be resources for thinking the Cloud in opposition to obsequious adherence to industry rationality, effective tools through which we can defy rhetoric aimed precisely at ensuring the Cloud remains unthought.

In particular, in attempting to end, we are reminded of *Inception*'s spinning top – Cobb's personal 'totem' which anchors its possessor to the world, which, as it topples, guarantees the dreams of others have been left behind, ensures a collapse of the state vector and an awakening to the actual. Of course, this totem is ultimately no guarantee at all since it is not itself secured against, dissociable from, the virtual realm. The film takes its leave with the image of the totem spinning, about to fall, but not falling. We are not in fact returned. The game is still in play. Similarly, our hopes of proposing some actual avenues of 'resistance' to the machinations of the Cloud dissipate. At this book's inception, when we *came to*, we found ourselves already traipsing around Penrose steps, already reactively enclosed in an unceasing loop. We wondered about a way out. As we contemplate this book's completion we find ourselves unable entirely to wake from the fever-dream of these fabulations. What strikes us is the impossibility of ending that litters what we have composed. Stranded still on the Penrose steps; or as if in Ballard's armoured

Crystal World, loaded up with time; or eating and eaten in Capital's ouroboric metaphysic; ensnared in the coils of the control society serpent; caught up within the cycle of infernal alternatives; chasing ghosts into even deeper caves; never cashing out; power, in its constructive instability, a prototype always falling. Irremediably, we are already Cloud natives, born of the digital Tentacular Novum, incarnations of weird ecology.

It's fitting, in fact, that one of the impossible endings we have touched upon takes place in the clouds. McCarthy's *Remainder* leaves off with the image of an aircraft turning out from an airport, then turning back again, banking one way and then the next, its vapour trails forming a figure eight, symbolic of the möbius-like infinity to a repeated, patterned sequence, an affective groove in which the narrator can slipstream himself. It calls to mind Howard Hughes, Paul Virilio's 'Master of Time', who, after piloting his aircraft around the world, lands and returns it to the precise spot from which he had departed, movement becoming inertia, end looped with beginning, everywhere and nowhere enclosed in disjunctive synthesis.

The impossible ending of *Remainder*, despite its acceleration into the hyperreal, preserves true pathos – the narrator admits that the closed loop performance of the aircraft's flight path is likely to face the problem of an empty fuel tank before the heat-death of the universe. The plane is actual, it will fall out of the sky, it will crash. But in *Inception*, we're denied any such entropy. Instead, Cobb's totemic spinning top is to be understood as actual-virtual, the perfect exemplar of constructive instability. The world of the Cloud continually quivers, as the spinning top does in the last microseconds of the film, but though it's always fall*ing*, the fall is never completed, there is no collapse. In *Inception*, the 'kick' is the point of exit, the jolt that brings us to. In military fabulation, the war story, this point of exit is 'extraction', the extraction point being the end of the mission, its successful completion; we similarly see this in video games, such as *Splinter Cell*, where extraction marks the completion of the level, a respite from action. *Inception* disallows this: just as in the security paradigm of the Cloud, the kick is the affect-drop, the manipulative stroke. The disjunctive synthesis of actual and virtual is also a disjunctive balancing act, a volatile maintenance, not of equilibrium but of constructive poise that continues to spin on and spin out worlding resonances. We make and perceive our world simultaneously. So in fact, the dynamism of these nonlinear resonances is precisely where its power lies; fluctuations in energy serving as unending fuel supply, a connected multitude of creative potential on-tap. This is a story with no clear beginning and no conceivable end, a dream, within a dream, within a dream ... And yet, despite all this, it is also a Hollywood movie and it will not quite let things pan out this way...

Noise has been central to our meditations. Discussing the ending of *Inception* between ourselves, the DVD not being to hand, we remembered it wrongly. In the actual ending, Cobb spins the top and steps into the garden to be reunited with his children. They turn to him, they have faces, they are real – he carries his faith within himself and he no longer needs the testimony of his totem. Ignored by Cobb, the sound the top makes suggests it has begun its topple, there is a sharp whine, and then both image and sound are cut. Black. Will it fall? Despite what we say above, we know that Yes, of course it will, insofar as Hollywood demands we keep the faith. In a bonus documentary on the DVD, Nolan even tells us so. But in our virtual, misremembered ending, the image may cut to black but we hear the top spin on. We prefer this ending. The noise that scrambles and belies what we end up saying, what faces turn towards us ... Nietzsche's ringing silence, before and beyond, refusing us the possibility of finality, of return, of ending, but in doing so, holding open the possibility of transformation. An echo, background noise, spinning a hide-out, concealing, incepting another future. Final and actual opinions? Mere totems of a stranger, richer world.

# References

## Inception

1    Elsaesser, T. (2009) 'The Mind-Game Film', in Buckland, W. (ed.) *Puzzle Films: Complex Storytelling in Contemporary Cinema*, Chichester: Wiley-Blackwell, p.39-40

2    See Lash, S. (2010) *Intensive Culture: Social Theory, Religion and Contemporary Capitalism*, London: Sage

3    Diken, B. (2009) *Nihilism*, London: Routledge

4    See numerous references to this by Slavoj Žižek

5    Ballard: 'I see elective psychopathology as *the coming thing*' in Vale, V. (ed.) (2005) *Conversations*, RE/Search, p.60

6    The technology the Inception team employ to break into the subconscious, we are informed in the movie, was originally developed as a military training programme before it (typically, of course) migrated into the corporate realm.

7    The concept of the virtual with which this book works is not the computer 'unreality' associated with debates around simulation, but rather, after Deleuze and others, refers to life's power of difference, as in the real but inactual state associated with, for example, the future.

## 1. The World Rights Itself

8    Evens, A. (2005) *Sound Ideas: Music, Machines, and Experience*, Minneapolis: University of Minnesota Press, p.69-70

9    Parikka, J. (2007) *Digital Contagions: A Media Archaeology of Computer Viruses*, New York: Peter Lang Publishing, p.72; Elsaesser, T. (2008) '"Constructive Instability", or: The Life of Things as the Cinema's Afterlife?' in G. Lovink & S. Niederer (eds.) (2008) *Video Vortex Reader: Responses to YouTube*, Amsterdam: Institute of Network Cultures

10   Marx, K. & Engels, F. (1969) 'Manifesto of the Communist Party', in Feuer, L.S. (ed.) *Marx and Engels: Basic Writings on*

*Politics and Philosophy*, London: Fontana, p. 53

11  Parikka, J. (2005) 'Digital Monsters, Binary Aliens – Computer Viruses, Capitalism and the Flow of Information' *Fibreculture*, vol.4 [online] Available at: http://www.fibre culture.org/journal/issue4/issue4_parikka.html

12  Leadbeater, C. (2010a) *Cloud Culture: The Future of Global Cultural Relations*, London: Counterpoint, p.23

13  Leadbeater, 2010a, p.21; p.54

14  Leadbeater, 2010a, p.78

15  Virno, P. (2004) *A Grammar of the Multitude*, Los Angeles/New York: Semiotext(e)/MIT Press, p.81

16  Hardt, M. (2009) 'The Common in Communism' [online]. Available at: http://seminaire.samizdat.net/The-Common-in-Communism.html

17  Leadbeater, C. (2010b) *Digging for the Future: An English Radical Manifesto*, London: The Young Foundation, p.37

18  Bernstein, E. (1963) *Cromwell and Communism: Socialism and Democracy in the Great English Revolution*, New York: Schocken, p.117

19  Winstanley cited in Hill, C. (1991) *The World Turned Upside Down: Radical Ideas During the English Revolution*, London: Penguin, p.137

20  Klein, N. (2008) *The Shock Doctrine: The Rise of Disaster Capitalism*, New York: Metropolitan/Henry Holt, p.303

21  Massumi, B. (2008) 'The Thinking-Feeling of What Happens' *Inflexions*, 1.1. 'How is Research-Creation?' [online] Available at: http://www.senselab.ca/inflexions/pdf/Massumi.pdf, p.2

22  Massumi, 2008, p.8

23  Massumi, 2008, p.9

24  Massumi, 2008, p.9

25  See Foucault, M. (1977) *Discipline and Punish: The Birth of the Prison*, London: Allen Lane

26  Deleuze, G. (1995) 'Postscript on Control Societies', *Negotiations*, New York: Columbia University Press, p.180

27   See Berardi, F. (2009) *Precarious Rhapsody: Semiocapitalism and the Pathologies of the Post-Alpha Generation*, London: Minor Compositions

28   Deleuze, G. (1995) 'Control and Becoming', *Negotiations*, New York: Columbia University Press, p.175. Further references in this paragraph to control societies are from this source.

29   Galloway, A. & Thacker, E. (2007) *The Exploit: A Theory of Networks*, Minneapolis: University of Minnesota Press, p.77

30   Galloway, A. (2006) *Gaming: Essays on Algorithmic Culture*, Minneapolis: University of Minnesota Press, p.90-91

31   Amit Singhal, Google programmer cited in Levy, S. (2010) 'How Google's Algorithm Rules the Web' *Wired* [Online] 22 February. Available at: http://www.wired.com/magazine /2010/02/ff_google_algorithm/

32   Quoted in Jenkins, H. W. (2010) 'Google and the Search for the Future' *Wall Street Journal* [Online] 14 August. Available at: http://online.wsj.com/article/SB10001424052748704901104575423294099527212.html

33   Hayles, N. K. (2006) 'Traumas of Code' *Critical Enquiry* vol.33, pp.136-157

34   Yet Hayles is careful to stress that this kind of control doesn't only take place in the dreamworld of the subconscious. In opposition to the un- or sub-conscious, she emphasizes the *nonconscious* and its effects on the extended cognitive system including bodily motor functions. We can think here of the millions of keystrokes, gestural movements across touch-screens, postures and ways of seeing, all of which become subtly entrained.

35   Leadbeater, C. (2010c) 'Apple and Google are pioneering "cloud capitalism". Should we be worried?' *The Observer*, 7 February, p.30

36   Deleuze, 1995, p.181

37   Fisher, M. (2001) 'SF Capital' *Transmat: Resources in*

*Transcendental Materialism* [online] Available at:
http://www.cinestatic.com/trans-mat/Fisher/sfcapital.htm.
All references to Fisher in this chapter are from this source
(no page numbers).

38 Lash, 2010, pp.131-154

39 Leadbeater, 2010a, p.28; Deleuze, G. (1988) *Foucault*, London:
Continuum, p.32

40 Miliband in Leadbeater, 2010a, p.10. The inception into
popular discourse of the Blairite terminology 'creative
industries' took place during New Labour's 1997 election
campaign; its use intensified throughout their term in
government, right up to their 'cultural manifesto' produced
prior to their defeat in 2010. The phrase has stuck. See The
Labour Party (2010) *Creative Britain: Labour's Cultural
Manifesto* and Garnham, N. (2005) 'From Cultural to Creative
Industries' *International Journal of Cultural Policy* vol.11 (1),
pp.15-29

41 Virno, 2004, pp.21-22

42 Virno, 2004, p.23

43 Leadbeater, 2010a, p.28

44 Miéville, C. (2009) 'Cognition as Ideology: A Dialectic of SF
Theory' in M. Bould & C. Miéville (eds.) *Red Planets: Marxism
and Science Fiction*, London: Pluto Press, p.238

45 This aide has now allegedly been identified as Bush's
Deputy Chief of Staff Karl Rove

46 Suskind, R. (2004) 'Faith, Certainty and the Presidency of
George W. Bush' *New York Times*, 17 October

47 Indeed, as Elmer and Opel point out, the 'absence of
evidence' can even be twisted into a reason for action,
decisions instead based on faith. Elmer, G. & Opel, A. (2008)
*Preempting Dissent: The Politics of an Inevitable Future*,
Winnipeg: Arbeiter Ring Publishing, p.24

48 Miéville, 2009, p.240

49 See Žižek, S. (2004) *Organs without Bodies: Deleuze and*

*Consequences*, London: Routledge, p.40

50 We can also note Žižek's observation that science and religion have effectively switched places, science providing the ontological and epistemological stability previously guaranteed by religion, although he argues that as science is granted a quasi-religious status (an accusation increasingly directed at Richard Dawkins), religion itself becomes a space of critical resistance. See Žižek, S. (2008) *Violence: Six Sideways Reflections*, New York: Picador, p.82

51 Cited in Hill, 1991, p.141

52 Hill, 1991, p.150

53 Virno, 2004, pp.110-111

54 Hardt & Negri, 2000, p.303. In their later work, Multitude, they change to using 'the common' rather than commons, in order to differentiate from the failed project of the past; their alternate terminology is aimed towards the future (see Hardt, M. & Negri, A. (2006) *Multitude: War and Democracy in the Age of Empire*, New York: Penguin Press)

55 Nietzsche, F. (2006) *On the Genealogy of Morality and Other Writings*, Cambridge: Cambridge University Press, p.36

56 Nietzsche, F. (2000) 'Beyond Good and Evil' in *Basic Writing of Nietzsche*, New York: Modern Library, p.419

## 2. Parasite Regime

57 Massumi, 2008

58 Massumi, 2008, p.5

59 Sylvester, D. (1993) *Interviews with Francis Bacon*, London: Thames & Hudson, p.17

60 Massumi, 2008, p.5

61 Massumi, 2008, p.19

62 Tiqqun (2010) *Introduction to Civil War*, Los Angeles: Semiotext(e), p.199-200

63 Elsaesser, 2008, p.20

64 Galloway, A. (2004) *Protocol: How Control Exists After*

*Decentralization*, Cambridge, Mass.: MIT Press, p.102

65  Kornbluh, A. (2010) 'On Marx's Victorian Novel', *Mediations* vol.25 (1) [online] Available at: http://www.mediationsjournal.org/articles/on-marx-s-victorian-novel

66  Marx, K. (1976) *Capital Volume 1*, London: Penguin, p.926

67  Marx, 1976, p.148

68  Marx, 1976, p.151

69  Kornbluh, 2010

70  Kornbluh, 2010

71  Elsaesser, 2008. References in this paragraph from pages 26-27

72  Galloway, 2004, p.113

73  Galloway, 2004, p.110

74  Chun, W.H.K. (2006) *Control and Freedom: Power and Paranoia in the Age of Fibre Optics*, Cambridge, Massachusetts: MIT Press, p.9

75  Nunes, M. (2011) 'Error, Noise, and Potential: The Outside of Purpose', in Nunes, M. (ed.) *Error: Glitch, Noise, and Jam in New Media Cultures*, London: Continuum, p.3

76  Nunes, 2011, p.12

77  Nunes, 2011, p.17

78  Nunes, 2011, pp.15-16

79  Galloway, 2004, p.17

80  Thrift, N. (2009) 'Pass it On: Towards a Political Economy of Propensity'. Conference paper delivered at the *Social Science and Innovation Conference*, Royal Society of the Arts, 11 February [online] Available at: http://www.aimresearch.org/uploads/File/Presentations/2009/FEB/NIGEL%20THRIFT%20PAPER.pdf, p.35

81  Pignarre, P. and Stengers, I. (2011) *Capitalist Sorcery: Breaking the Spell*, Houndmills: Palgrave Macmillan

82  Fisher, M. (2009) *Capitalist Realism: Is There No Alternative?* Winchester: 0 Books

83  Diken, 2009. In general, our perspective on nihilism is

indebted to this volume.

84   Pignarre and Stengers, 2011, p.22

85   Pignarre and Stengers, 2011, p.28

86   Dyer-Witheford, N. (1999) *Cyber-Marx*, Urbana and Chicago: University of Illinois Press, p.68

87   Hardt & Negri, 2006

88   Goffey, A. (2011) 'Introduction: On the Witch's Broomstick'' in Pignarre and Stengers, p.xvi-xvii

89   Lanier, J. (2011) *You Are Not A Gadget*, London: Penguin, p.188

90   Miéville, C. (2008) 'M.R. James and the Quantum Vampire: Weird; Hauntological: Versus and/or and and/or or?' *Collapse: Philosophical Research and Development*, vol.IV, p.105

91   Miéville, 2008, p.128

92   Brassier, R. & Ieven, B. (2009) 'Transitzone/Against an Aesthetics of Noise', *nY* [online] http://www.ny-web.be/transitzone/against-aesthetics-noise.html

93   Hardt & Negri, 2006, p.196

94   Shaviro, S. (2008) 'Monstrous Flesh', *The Pinocchio Theory*, 17 June [Blog] Available at: http://www.shaviro.com/Blog/?p=639

95   Shaviro, S. (2008) 'The Body of Capital', *The Pinocchio Theory*, 20 June [Blog] Available at: http://www.shaviro.com/Blog/?p=641

96   In terms of developments in weird fiction, it is perhaps not coincidental that new additions to Lovecraft's Cthulhu Mythos include a collection entitled *Cthulhu's Reign* (ed. Darrell Schweitzer, 2010), the focus of which is on what happens when the Old Ones finally break through, once Cthulhu has risen and is fully abroad in the world. In Mike Allens' contribution to the volume, 'Her Acres of Pastoral Playground', the protagonist attempts to preserve the fiction of a pocket of order amidst the chaos, but is ultimately left with no illusion about the status of his

sanctum: 'Inside your shell, time still flows forward, but that time will end. Outside, time is still. Outside, your future is now. Outside, you are with us and have been forever and will be forever. Your future is now' (p.70).

97 Ballmer, S. (2010) 'Seizing the Opportunity of the Cloud: The Next Wave of Business Growth' [Transcript of Public Lecture] 5 October. Available at: http://www2.lse.ac.uk/publicEvents/events/2010/20101005t0830vSZT.aspx.

98 Fuller, M. (2005) *Media Ecologies: Materialist Energies in Art and Technoculture*, Cambridge, Mass.: MIT Press, p.2; p.4, our emphasis

99 Elsaesser, 2008, p.17

100 Foucault, M. (2003) *Society Must Be Defended: Lectures at the Collège de France, 1975-76*, New York: Picador, p.243

101 Foucault, 2003, p.244

102 Foucault, 2003, p.246; p.249

103 Foucault, 2003, p.245

104 Hardt & Negri, 2006, p.192, our emphasis

105 Serres, M. (1982) *The Parasite*, Baltimore and London: John Hopkins University Press, p.5

106 Serres, 1982, p.51

107 Serres, 1982, p.7

108 Foucault, 2003, p.245

109 We were first pointed to this text by Jussi Parikka's reference to it in *Digital Contagions* (2007)

110 Edwards, P. (1996) *The Closed World: Computers and the Politics of Discourse in Cold War America*, Cambridge, Mass.: MIT Press, p.9

111 Edwards, 1996, p.308

112 Berners-Lee, T. (2000) *Weaving the Web: The Past, Present and Future of the World Wide Web by its Inventor*, London & New York: Texere, p.171. The underlying rhetoric here is of the much discussed 'noosphere' – the Cloud as collaborative brain.

113 Galloway, 2004, p.75

114 Parikka, 2007, p.27, n.9

115 Fuller, 2005, p.173

116 Serres, 1982, p.95

117 Edwards, 1996, p.12

118 Edwards, 1996, p.13

119 Edwards, 1996, p.312

120 Deleuze, G. & Parnet, C. (1987) *Dialogues*, New York: Colombia University Press, p.56

121 Nietzsche, 2006, p.550

122 Serres, 1982, p.96

123 Serres, 1982, p.52

124 O'Reilly, T. & Battelle, J. (2009) 'Web Squared: Web 2.0 Five Years On', pp.2-4

125 Brennan, T. (2004) *The Transmission of Affect*, London: Cornell University Press, p.1

126 Serres, 1982, pp.52-3

127 Shouse, E. (2005) 'Feeling, Emotion, Affect' *M/C Journal* [online] vol.8 (6), December. Available at: http://journal .media-culture.org.au/0512/03-shouse.php

128 Shouse, 2005

129 Berardi, 2009

130 The notion of 'worlding' used here is that employed by Maurizio Lazzarato and Nigel Thrift.

131 Thrift, 2009, pp.29-32

132 Lanier, J. (2010) 'On the Threshold of the Avatar Era' *The Wall Street Journal* [Online] 23 October. Available at: http://online.wsj.com/article/SB10001424052702303738504575568410584865010.html

133 See Thrift, N. (2008) *Non-Representational Theory: Space, Politics, Affect*, Oxon: Routledge

134 Thrift, 2008, p.186

135 Doane, M. A. (2002) *The Emergence of Cinematic Time: Modernity, Contingency, the Archive*, Cambridge, Mass.:

Harvard University Press, p.46. Chronophotography also anticipated the development of cinema.

136 Thrift, 2008, p.186. This notion of bodily anticipation was explicitly theorized in the Nineteenth century by Wilhelm Wundt and Hermann von Helmholtz, the latter of whom directly proposed that self consciousness 'lagged behind the present'. This was later formalized by Benjamin Libet.

137 Massumi, B. (2002) *Parables of the Virtual: Movement, Affect, Sensation*, Durham & London, Duke University Press, p.28

138 Thrift, 2008, p.186; our emphasis

139 The tag line to *Inception* is 'Your Mind is the Scene of the Crime'

140 'There is no true or real "reality" – "Reality" is simply a more or less constant scanning pattern – The scanning pattern we accept as "reality" has been imposed by the controlling power on this planet, a power primarily oriented towards total control.' Burroughs, W. S. (1992) *Nova Express*, New York: Grove, p.53

141 Hardt & Negri, 2006, p.198

142 Stiegler, B. (2010) *For a New Critique of Political Economy*, Cambridge: Polity Press, pp.31-3

143 Goodman, S. (2008) 'Audio Virology: On the Sonic Mnemonics of Preemptive Power' in C. Birdsall and A. Enns (eds.) *Sonic Mediations: Body, Sound, Technology*, Cambridge: Cambridge Scholars, p.32

144 Serres, p.122

145 Lefebvre, H. (2004) *Rhythmanalysis: Space, Time and Everyday Life*, London: Continuum

146 Ballard, J. G. (1974) 'Introduction to the French edition of *Crash!*' Available at: http://www.jgballard.ca/interviews/louit_interview1974.html

147 Massumi, B. (1992) *A User's Guide to Capitalism and Schizophrenia*, Cambridge, Mass.: MIT Press, p.135

148 Massumi, 2002, p.29

149 Wiener, N. (1954) *The Human Use of Human Beings: Cybernetics and Society*, Boston: Da Capo Press, p.33

150 Goodman, 2008, p.34

151 Goodman, S. (2010) *Sonic Warfare: Sound, Affect, and the Ecology of Fear*, Cambridge, Massachusetts: MIT Press, p.123

152 Burroughs, W. S. (2001) 'Origin and Theory of the Tape Cut-Ups' *Break Through in Grey Room* [Album] Track 2, Sub Rosa Records

## 3. Reverse Obsolescence

153 Bell, G. & Gemmell, J. (2009) *Total Recall: How the E-Memory Revolution Will Change Everything*, USA: Dutton/Penguin, p.46

154 Bell & Gemmell, 2009, p.14. The researchers acknowledge that the themes concerning the Total Recall project have been explored previously in SF – they mention the novel *Hominids* by Robert J. Sawyer, the Robin Williams film *Final Cut* and even the British sitcom *Red Dwarf* (pp.16-17). Tellingly though, given their unequivocal method of dealing with 'problems' of memory by applying a business model, they fail to make any mention of the film with which their project shares its name and which itself was originally adapted from the Philip K. Dick novel *We Can Remember It For You Wholesale*. Given the fact that Dick is so incisive in his writing on memory, this is perhaps hardly surprising.

155 Terminology derived from Connerton, P. (2009) *How Modernity Forgets*, Cambridge: Cambridge University Press, p.146. Connerton also notes that the European cult of monuments and the funding for public museums both accelerated greatly with the age of mechanical reproduction. In the mnemotechnological era – the 'digital revolution' – memory becomes an even greater socio-cultural force, the Cloud taking on the role of systemically integrated *museum of totality* (p.27).

156  Bell & Gemmell, 2009, p.60

157  Nietzsche, F. (1997) 'On the Uses and Disadvantages of History for Life' in *Untimely Meditations*, Cambridge: Cambridge University Press, p.62

158  'There has never been a document of culture, which is not simultaneously one of barbarism' Benjamin, W. (1970) *Illuminations*, London: Jonathan Cape, p.258

159  Nietzsche, (1997), p.62

160  Smithson, R. (1996) 'Entropy and the New Monuments' in J. Flam (ed.) *Robert Smithson: The Collected Writings*, Berkeley: University of California Press. Also archived at: http://www.robertsmithson.com/essays/entropy_and.htm

161  Bell & Gemmell, 2009, p.5, p.6, p.8

162  Derrida, J. (1996) *Archive Fever: A Freudian Impression*, Chicago: University of Chicago Press, pp.16-17

163  Bell & Gemmell, 2009, p.23

164  Bell & Gemmell, 2009, p.165

165  Bell & Gemmell, 2009, p.166

166  On this point, see Goodman, S. & Parisi, L. (2010) 'Machines of Memory' in S. Radstone & B. Schwarz (eds.) *Memory: Histories, Theories, Debates*, New York: Fordham University Press, p.345

167  Bell & Gemmell, 2009, p.58

168  Bell & Gemmell, 2009, p.144, our emphasis; p.145

169  Handke, P. (1972) *The Goalie's Anxiety at the Penalty Kick*, New York: Rarrar, Straus and Giroux, pp.132-3

170  Perec, G. (2010) *An Attempt at Exhausting a Place in Paris*, Cambridge, Massachusetts: Wakefield Press

171  Perec, G. (1997) 'Approaches to What?' in *Species of Spaces and Other Pieces*, Harmondsworth: Penguin, pp.205-7. 'Make an inventory of your pockets,' Perec suggests, 'Question your tea spoons.'

172  Perec, 2010

173  Henri Pireon cited in Connerton, 2009, p.86

174  Bell & Gemmell, 2009, p.28

175  Bell & Gemmell, 2009, p.6

176  Bell & Gemmell, 2009, p.154

177  For his complete vision, see Kurzeil, R. (2005) *The Singularity is Near: When Humans Transcend Biology*, Viking Press. The standardization of the GPS-enabled device combined with the increasing ubiquity of the RFID chip and rapid developments in augmented reality accelerates an already algorithmic thinking. Not only will the Cloud ecology soon remind us to buy milk when we've run out (making recommendations for action before we're aware action is necessary) it will increasingly utilize the distributed data-slurry of our lives to feed back a pattern for productive efficiency, a modulating pattern that, in the face of increasingly complex chances for resistance, will be passively followed. As Steven Shaviro puts it, "[a]n orientation towards the future – even, or especially, towards an incomprehensible one – must alter your behaviour in the present" (Shaviro, S. (2009) 'The Singularity is Here' in M. Bould & C. Miéville (eds.) *Red Planets: Marxism and Science Fiction*, London: Pluto Press, p.105).

178  Shaviro, 2009, p.105

179  Lanier, 2011, p.26

180  Thrift, 2008, p.31

181  Amoore, L. (2009) 'Algorithmic War: Everyday geographies of the war on terror' *Antipode: Journal of Radical Geography* vol.41 (1), p.56

182  Responding to a question relating to a 'report of no evidence', Rumsfeld stated: 'Reports that say that something hasn't happened are always interesting to me, because as we know, there are known knowns; there are things we know we know. And we also know there are known unknowns; that is to say we know there are some things we do not know. But there are also unknown

unknowns – the ones we don't know we don't know.' Rumsfeld, D. & Myers, R. (2002) Department of Defense News Briefing, Feb 12. Available at: http://www.defense. gov/transcripts/transcript.aspx?transcriptid=2636. Rumsfeld has seemingly embraced his media persona as the Yoda of neo-liberal militarism, even giving his 2011 autobiography the title 'Known and Unknown'.

183 Wolfowitz, P. (2001) 'Were We Asleep?' [Department of Defense memo to D. Rumsfeld] Sept 18, cited in Kean, T. H. et al. (2004) *The 9/11 Commission Report*, National Commission on Terrorist Attacks upon the United States, p.559, n.75

184 Kean et al., 2004, p.344

185 Wolfowitz, P. (2001) 'Preventing More Events' [Department of Defense Memo to D. Rumsfeld] Sept 17, cited in Kean et al., 2004, p.559, n.74. Wolfowitz argued that if there were even a 10 percent chance of Saddam Hussein's guilt in coordinating the 9/11 attacks (and he believed the odds greater than this), "maximum priority should be placed on *eliminating the threat...*" pp.335-6; our emphasis.

186 Kean et al., 2004, p.408

187 Amoore, 2009, p.52

188 See Martin, R. (2007) *An Empire of Indifference: American War and the Financial Logic of Risk Management*, Durham and London: Duke University Press

189 Massumi, B. (2010) 'The Future Birth of the Affective Fact: The Political Ontology of Threat' in M. Gregg & G.J. Seigworth (eds.) *The Affect Theory Reader*, Durham & London: Duke University Press, pp.52-70

190 Grusin, R. (2010) *Premediation: Affect and Mediality after 9/11*, Great Britain: Palgrave Macmillan, p.8

191 A 'wild riot of pointless imaginings' John Wyndham (author of *Day of the Triffids*) cited in Sawyer, A. (2009) 'Space Opera' in M. Bould et al (eds.) *The Routledge Companion to Science*

*Fiction*, London & New York: Routledge, p.506. On the energizing potential of psychopathology, see Ballard, J.G. (2005) *Conversations*, San Francisco, CA: RE/Search, p.100

192 Elsaesser, 2009, pp.13-41

193 *Heroes* features characters with various pathological powers (Nikki Sanders is quite literally a split-personality) but again the focus is often on the issue of temporality, explored through the characters of Hiro Nakamura with his ability to time travel and junky-artist Isaac Mendez who can paint the future when high. In what seems to be almost a moral message concerning the danger in breaking temporal linearity or causality, the use of special powers is depicted to be not only addictive but further results in the character deteriorating physically in health and strength.

194 Elsaesser, 2009, p.19

195 Elsaesser, 2009, p.21

196 Goodman & Parisi, p.345

197 Massumi, B. (2005) 'Fear (The Spectrum Said)' *Positions* vol.13 (1)

198 Deleuze, G. & Guattari, F. (2004) *Anti-Oedipus*, London: Continuum, p.38. Jonathan Beller also discusses a similar new mode of production that co-opts inventive deviance and our 'bouts with psychopathology' in order to intuit 'glitches' in the system, to securely expand the reaches of what is accepted as 'reality'.

199 Elsaesser, 2009, p.29

200 Noys, B. (2009) 'Better Living through Psychopathology' Presentation at 'The Future', David Roberts Art Foundation, 5 November. Transcript available at: http://www.ballar dian.com/better-living-through-psychopathology

201 Grusin, 2010, p.35. Here we are leaning on but not specifically adopting Grusin's concept of 'premediation'.

202 McCarthy, T. (2007) *Remainder*, Surrey: Alma Books, p.23

203 McCarthy, 2007, p.62

204  McCarthy, 2007, p.76

205  Deleuze, G. (1989) *Cinema 2: The Time Image*, London: Continuum, p.80

206  Bergson cited in Deleuze, 1989, p.77

207  'Time was condensing around him, a thousand replicas of himself from the past and future had invaded the present and clasped themselves to him' Ballard, J. G. (2006) 'Myths of the Near Future' in *The Complete Short Stories: Volume 2*, London: Harper Perennial, p.621

208  Ballard, 2006, p.626

209  Bell & Gemmell, 2009, pp.55-57

210  Ballard, 2005, p.122

211  Derrida, J. (1994) *Specters of Marx: The State of Debt, the Work of Mourning and the New International*, New York & London: Routledge

212  Bell & Gemmell, 2009, p.4

213  Del Pilar Blanco, M. & Peeren, E. (eds.) (2010) *Popular Ghosts: The Haunted Spaces of Everyday Culture*, London: Continuum, pp.xiii-xiv

214  McCarthy, 2007, p.135

215  McCarthy, 2007, pp.184-5

216  McCarthy, 2007, p.210

217  McCarthy, 2007, p.219

218  See, for example, McCarthy, 2007, p.160

Contemporary culture has eliminated both the concept of the
public and the figure of the intellectual. Former public spaces –
both physical and cultural – are now either derelict or colonized
by advertising. A cretinous anti-intellectualism presides,
cheerled by expensively educated hacks in the pay of
multinational corporations who reassure their bored readers
that there is no need to rouse themselves from their interpassive
stupor. The informal censorship internalized and propagated by
the cultural workers of late capitalism generates a banal
conformity that the propaganda chiefs of Stalinism could only
ever have dreamt of imposing. Zer0 Books knows that another
kind of discourse – intellectual without being academic, popular
without being populist – is not only possible: it is already
flourishing, in the regions beyond the striplit malls of so-called
mass media and the neurotically bureaucratic halls of the
academy. Zer0 is committed to the idea of publishing as a
making public of the intellectual. It is convinced that in
the unthinking, blandly consensual culture in which we live,
critical and engaged theoretical reflection is more important
than ever before.